DUNL

Est: Collected reports from

***

Edited by

MW Bewick and Ella Johnston

Est: Collected reports from East Anglia

Published by Dunlin Press in 2015

Dunlin Press
Wivenhoe, Essex
dunlinpress.com | @dunlinpress

ISBN: 978-0-9931259-0-4

A CIP record of this book is available from the British Library.

Printed in Great Britain by Ingram Spark.

Set in Garamond Pro.

Cover illustration and design by Ella Johnston.

CONTENTS

Foreword: Driving East

The parallel run of A1 and M11 motorways divides England as effectively as any border zone: to the west the undulating urban and suburban sprawl and the familiar rural; to the east the flatlands, reclaimed from the sea, and, being reclaimed by the sea, an unadorned Puritan landscape, horizon bisecting country and sky like a child's drawing. Of these parts it is said there's no climate, only a succession of weather: huge, cinematic skies and revolutionary winds.

The east traditionally stands for lost causes. It is what gets left behind in the migratory drift west. England ignores East Anglia, on the way to nowhere. Everything to the right of the M11 and A1 is ceded. Most of it doesn't even look like it belongs to the rest of the country and in appearance, architectural influence, irrigation systems and agricultural and horticultural intent can be more like Holland or Germany.

I was aware of East Anglia from an early age because my father was an officer in the Royal Norfolk Regiment and I landed up in Norwich, posted there from an army garrison in a small town in Germany in 1958. Norfolk felt different because my arrival had already been marked by the unwelcome transition of being sent away to school, putting me in the strange position of being homesick that first term for a place I had yet to see.

I also used to come this way a lot in the spring of 1981,

leaving London early and driving against the traffic up the M11 then down empty roads across country to explore the western Fens and the remotest areas of the Wash.

Today, driving towards the edge of the Fens, the sky grows immense. The light sharpens and assaults the eye. This light is unmatched anywhere else in England, proof available in the nineteenth-century schools of painting that struggled to catch its qualities. On days like these, East Anglia is all exhilaration. But a history of depression lurks, subject to the pathetic fallacy: clear one day, shrouded in gloom the next; it is hard hereabouts for mood not to be dominated by the sky.

I drift east, driving on into that zone of being between two points and out of reach, when the road, framed by the windscreen, becomes like a movie. Driving and cinema are both forms of controlled projection capable of freeing the mind; the car and movie theatre are among the last spaces of secular meditation and retreat.

Driving through countryside vaguely remembered and profoundly forgotten, landscape and memory merge. I half expect to overtake and glimpse in the rear-view mirror the frowning child I once was, walking down the road. A place unvisited for almost a lifetime becomes like only yesterday. Time accelerates. We drive into cliché.

After heading further east again, at Southwold, estuaries start to break up the coastline. The road is resisted. Detours become a feature. Driving on past an interesting run of beach houses between Thorpeness and Aldeburgh, including one used in Peter Greenaway's film *A Zed and Two Noughts*. To the south, Orford and Orford Ness.

Orford Castle is where Michael Reeves filmed the ending of that most cultish English film, *Witchfinder General*, starring a novice Ian Ogilvy and campy old Vincent Price, who was put up in the Dickens suite at the Angel hotel in Bury St Edmunds. The film remains a rarity in commercial English cinema for its use of locations and cinematic understanding of landscape and movement.

The drives I made in 1981 were for a film I intended to shoot on location because this whole landscape remains the most cinematic, as opposed to picturesque, that we have. I wanted to use its flatness as a way of eliminating class nuance, the bane of English cinema, but budget restrictions meant everything got shot in the Home Counties, effectively killing the point.

Because I was never able to film all this landscape I put it in fiction instead: a killing at Denver Sluice, sodden fields, a posthumous journey through rising floods, a car dowsed in a canal, a red telephone box in an empty landscape.

People make little impression in this reclaimed emptiness, much flooded and awaiting future deluges. The East Anglian land defines itself as the opposite of romantic, more in terms of suspense and the threat that comes with emptiness. It is no place for souvenir postcards. It just is.

Chris Petit

Introduction

The reports that comprise this book were collected during the summer of 2014 and concern East Anglia. But this book is also not about East Anglia. It is about people, history, memories, possible futures, alternate realities. And yet much of what follows describes places in East Anglia, or is written by contributors based in East Anglia.

Indeed, the very notion of this book arose during a well-tramped walk through Dedham Vale – off the London to Norwich train at Manningtree and past Flatford Mill, the aspic heart of Constable Country, to Dedham village and a lunchtime meal at the Sun Inn. Over a bottle of wine, the idea for the project gradually took shape: to ask people with an interest in East Anglia to write about the region in whatever way they liked, be that poetry, reportage or anything else. The result was to be a psychogeography of the region (according to one of us that day) or a time capsule (according to the other) – a record of thought about the region at a moment in time.

The contributions selected to be in in this volume arrived via an open submissions process. Word was put out at the region's universities, via social media, in the pub with friends, and through professional connections. Contributions arrived from Norfolk, Suffolk, Cambridgeshire and, in large quantities, from Essex. It led to a question: where does East Anglia begin and where does it end?

Historically, Cambridgeshire, Norfolk and Suffolk are the counties that constitute East Anglia, a mapping that sees its western limits almost touch Peterborough and the fringes of central England. But what of Essex, the ancient Anglo-Saxon kingdom that forms the middle ground between lands of the North Folk and South Folk and London to the south?

Geologically, East Anglia is part of the scarplands of southeast England where muds, clays, sands, limestones and chalk from the Jurassic and Cretaceous periods were deposited. The region's boundary is easy to define to the northwest at the Fens and the chalk of the East Anglian Heights – part of a great ridge that runs southwest all the way to Dorset. But East Anglia's southern boundary is less distinct as the land slips inexorably into the tertiary sands, gravels and clays of the London basin and the trough of the Thames.

Today, the transport links that push London's growing population overspill out to the furthest reaches of East Anglia also cement Essex's place as a de facto past of East Anglia's human geography. The faces of Billericay, Harwich, as well as Sheringham, Ely, Norwich, Ipswich, Woodbridge and Sudbury, all congregate and exchange frustrated glances on the concourse of Liverpool Street Station, if trains ferrying commuters out to 'Greater Anglia' are delayed during the evening's rush hour.

East Anglia: that great half-heart-shape of land that stretches from the Wash to the Thames and from the Fens to what has sometimes been known as the German Sea. This highly cultivated arable land delivers good yields of wheat, roots, fruit and barley from paradoxically infertile soils – the poor sandy soils of the Cromer Ridge, the dry earth of Breckland and the wet clays of Essex.

This collection reports back from that land. Its yield is wide-ranging: a wanderer tramps Suffolk's shingle beaches; a folk-singing academic remembers a musical past; Colchester burns again; today's poor make their way to a food bank; Old Shuck patrols the Norfolk sands; echoes of war reverberate; a painter's canvas is carefully unfurled across the marsh; we glimpse wrecks of boats, motels and roads; someone stares at a rutted field; we dig, and we dig again, searching for clues to personal histories and the history of the region.

At a gallery talk by one of the contributors to this volume, the artist Luke Elwes, a question was raised as to his method of painting landscape. In an eloquent and thoughtful response, Elwes described how in his work he attempts to avoid the "tyranny of the horizon". What does this mean? It means, perhaps, that as an artist he is not seeking to produce work that represents a totality of viewpoint.

Horizons mark the edge. They encourage the definitive. With *Est* we too wanted to avoid totalities. This is no definitive account of an East Anglian geography or sensibility. Indeed, what this collection demonstrates is nothing more than what East Anglia possibly might have been like in the minds of some writers at a certain moment. There is nothing definite here. What suggests fact or reality is hardly more than a surreality. The reports are a circumlocution of a land that both exists and does not exist. They look outward to the Continent and beyond; inward to an empty hinterland. They are about East Anglia, and they are not.

Brahms and the Angels

The Church of Our Lady Saint Mary, South Creake

On the altar dais,
the string quartet
before the rood screen crowned
by Christ Crucified
bring Brahms into the white walled pillared church.

September light, bright
through diamond panes
dapples the first violin,
splashes over
the locked counterpoint of viola and cello.

Leaves spin and fall outside,
while here in this scented space
the strings spill Autumn, whose notes
float upwards,
winning praise from the painted angels.

Seraphim unstinting
in their given task
to hold
and bear aloft
the ancient timbered roof.

Peter Kennedy

The Empty Quarter

Place possesses us. Place colonises us. It is a dirt simple, soil simple truth that we so often deny. For years I found it hard to tell the difference between the terrible warping gravity of nostalgia and the constant pull of the county of my childhood.

Every time I went back to Essex I was worried I would just find myself orbiting dead nexuses. Taking all the cognitive shortcuts of nostalgia that divorce you from your own history, walk you into an opium fog of false recollection.

Yet Essex was a constant tax on my memory. A call to flow down the Thames. Past the failed Quatermass futures glimpsed in cooling towers and sky gouge of the Coryton Refinery. To drift out to where the sunken time bomb of the SS Richard Montgomery threatens the vision punching neon of Southend's seafront. To let my feet trace contours set down by the retreat of ice.

The more maligned the country of my childhood has become, the more misrepresented by faux reality media and approved experts such as Jonathan Meades, the greater the need to return. To let it speak to me directly. To hear its voice in the clear acts of being there, walking it.

If I needed to listen to my birthplace, there was a specific route to be followed. An X on my own internal chart to be achieved. Fenchurch Street to Southchurch, the push north via Wallasea. Then the full expedition to the Empty Quarter.

Cartographers only ever extended it the title of Dengie Peninsula. They gave it official borders – River Crouch to the south; Blackwater to the north; old Dengie Hundred line to west; Germanic sea as eastern reach – but missed its true definition. They marked marshes on paper, projected the major tide streams, but never caught its secret name. The truth is only revealed by those who traipse it, those who live there. The Empty Quarter is folk irony. Devoid of hills, so few people at times you could easily imagine it as apocalypse backdrop, yet mystery dense and ghost swarmed. Nowhere fuller of forgotten corners.

I made the decision. I stopped fighting Essex. Left London in reverse shots. A train window movie rewind. Collapsed lungs of gasometer bones. Walls sigilised with graffiti. Pulled backwards through a mesmerising blur of unravelling industrial estates, car graveyards and haunted concrete. City losing cohesion at its ragged borders. Stuttering out, unable to find its place on the page, its story ending long before the official psychic marker of the M25.

The train takes me under the magic circle and into the rush of everyday Essex. A parade of uncurated copses, flooded farmland holding a mirror to a migraine sky, Homesteads stalked by pylons. The train now showing a film of place adrift in time. I could be moving through any decade of my own past. The county has always looked this way to me. Choked ditches failing to drain fields sodden with history of seed and plough. Hedges running with glee to the crowns of unambitious hills. Playgrounds of abandoned clay, heavy with possibility.

The track begins to flirt with water. I catch the flames of Canvey's refineries, burning like memorial candles for those who died in the flood of 1953. Between Leigh and Chalkwell the waves almost touch the carriage. A mist is fleeing the Thames estuary. Sky, sea and land becoming enmeshed. Everything drawn from the same palette of battle-weary greys.

Punching through this confusion is the solid form of the former HMS Wilton. A dead minehunter enduring an afterlife moored in the limbo between Thames and North Sea. Distilled naval drabness. The 'plastic pig' was the world's first warship made of glass-reinforced plastic. Its construction designed to reduce its magnetic signature. In this colour hypoxia, its greyout camouflage keeps it invisible to the last moment.

Before Wilton, the mooring was taken by the Bembridge, a 1930s pilot tender and Dunkirk hero. Plucky amateur battler being replaced with hardened professional warrior whilst my back was turned on the old patch.

The change forces me to remember furtive childhood exploring of the Bembridge. My fear at being caught as thick as the smell of dead engine oil. The stealthiest of steps still producing wooden creaks and metallic echoes.

The ship was a highlight of winter walks along the shore path from Old Leigh to Westcliff. Every step of the journey accompanied by a pulsing beat of rigging forced to slap mast by the wind. The pack of dinghies, stored on wooden jetties till spring, provided the most intense rhythmic chorus. When I got my first watch at the age of seven, I used to hold it to my ear. I could free myself from whatever was troubling me by listening to the workings. I did not hear tick-tock, I heard magic. I marvelled at how the thing on my wrist captured the sound of the boats and bluster.

I leave the train two stations short of the end of the line. Get out to find Southchurch is under migraine weather. Sky bruised black with premature darkness. Constant static of cold, spiteful rain. A thousand instant craters spluttering in and out of existence on the platform. A fluid lunarscape.

Skin tightens to armour under the barrage of water needles. The relentless imitation of monsoon bullies me into getting a bus to Paglesham. Proper exploration of the spiv diaspora of Southend and its suburbs will wait for another day. I settle for the occulted ley line route of the Number 60, snaking through edge estates to a subdued agricultural landscape where punctuation is provided by occasional brutal stabs of industrial building. Functional barns, silos and depots all brandishing relentless hostility to weather through breeze-block and corrugated iron.

At times like this you are thankful for this country's

remaining bursts of pub culture. Time and roof to wait out the rain. The true spirit houses of England. Two old men smoke in the cover of The Plough and Sail. Guarding its doors like an ale-addled Gog and Magog, trading burnt-out futures. Before they and their wheezed out cigarette phantoms will let you through into the dry, passwords are needed. A traditional combination of nods and dull, stared intent.

A pint and a half later and the roaring streams of water outside have eased. I venture outside, make my way to Church End. Walk round the bone yard of St Peter's, find the psychic skin of the place dissolved like blotting paper. Shades of the past mobbing me, trying to get close enough to tell me their stories. As I look through windows to bloated orange pumpkins, remnants of harvest festival, I can see a burst of blue hope caught in the glass. This is last of hærfest. This is autumn's dead frontier. It can go no further. Failing and falling, the year is on its knees and waiting for the sword of winter.

I walk into empty Essex. Fields that run towards the clouds, run towards the lip of the land. Out here, narrative loses its momentum. Wind-lashed, it becomes disorientated in creek and marsh. Even the rivers Roach and Crouch become confused, experiencing identity crises as they cross the liminal salt borders of estuary.

The sky swings low, scoops with open arms as I reach Wallasea. My ears are full of the rhythmic slap breeze bullied rigging from craft abandoned till spring. It is a sound of home, of the past. I walk amid brine-scarred hulks of wood and iron. Dead boats and jetties left to the oblivion of mud and rot. Stripped of purpose and identification, it is impossible to know if they are foundlings or sacrifices to the weather.

The tawdry Essex myths of bling and tan break apart on the jagged edge of England. Mythology of dark lantern and sea witch is reasserted. Shucks pad along the sea walls, hunt for bones in the spoil from Crossrail's tunnel which has been shipped in to stretch the island further into the sea. Here where England ends, London's spoil becomes Essex's expansion. The city's surplus thrown down to become new edgeland, new liberty to have rumour projected upon.

Walking the Empty Quarter is a dance with its spirits. Open yourself to the memories soaked into clay and they whisper to you. Engage with the history staked below the flow of certain crossroads and you can listen to stories that were old to the Legio XIV Gemina. This is a ghost kingdom, an ectoplasm zone. A place of lost time. Dead time. Reflections are bruised in sump pools that bleed rumour. Tramp its length to read a grimoire of possible realities.

A journey here, no matter how banal its purpose, cuts into history. Traipsing down almost path, you can kick up anecdotes. Cunning Essex, crow doctor Essex is just a foot scuff away from those walking its corpse lanes. You can learn all the secret languages of Dengie by moving through it. All of the hidden tongues of the region accessible to those who walk.

Mud on the Doc Martens and the salt burn kiss of wind teach you lessons quickly. Remind you there are maps tattooed on your bones, genetic circuit diagrams of where you grew up that kick into life as soon your feet put sparks into them. Lessons that force you to accept we are products of landscape, our stories so entwined with its narratives that to think of them as separate is a form of mental illness.

As I push on, mobile phone coverage becomes asthmatic. The wheezing up and down of the signal strength indicator monitors the last gasps of the twenty-first century before a glorious silence is imposed. On the marsh I navigate by lines. Walk under leys marked by telegraph poles. Track wire corridors. Direction from the songline hum of pylons that march to the unwanted science fictions of Bradwell.

Left-handed towers, sinister in every sense, hold up threads humming dread. The sentient metal giants that walked the fields of childhood imagination, mark trajectories of leukaemia paranoia. *Edge of Darkness* conspiracies manifest in the square-box shadow of unwanted Magnox and the possibility of new reactors. Here at the mouth of the Blackwater, shades are a crowd. Ghosts from the dead future of white hot technology mourn the swimming they once enjoyed in the warm water outflow of Reactor A.

In this terrain, you feel the pull of landmark gravity

more keenly. Even the obsolete drags you across the mire, across the mud. Fossil spaces – buildings that outlived their original purpose – still sing songs of their former lives. We march to them not to find shelter nor succour, but something of ourselves. Something lost. What was forgotten in the static of the city, now waiting on the horizon as derelict memories. Ready to be walked to, ready for conversation with us. Ready to live in our imagination.

I take the last line left to me. The old way to St. Peter's Chapel. As the footsteps rack up, they take it from Roman road to beaten up track and finally, the only certain path through marsh. Treading turf, buffeted by bullying wind, I want to run to the security of its walls. However, my feet have failed me. Swollen and sore, I can only trudge on. A pilgrim not to God, but to the faith in place.

A church has stood here for more than 1,500 years, East Saxons harvesting material from the legion fort of Othona to build sharp walls to keep the storms at bay. A sacred castle able to survive any weather siege. Inside I read tales in the Braille of Roman brick and stone. Listen as the wind still finds its way through the millennia old cracks in the building's fabric.

I allow myself to be possessed again. Being in the Dengie Hundred calls out to information stored deep in my DNA museum. Primal recognition is everywhere. It is in the wind and tide carved mud; in vegetation flinching from brutal sea born storms. This was the place, this is the place. The landscape reminds you it is older than Essex, older than any builder on it. Slaps you around till you feel man as pismire. A collapsing moment, a chalk pattern on shale that will not last the coming winter.

At the lip of Essex, at the end of England, we have reached the edge of national narrative. Confronted by the foreign sea, it stammers and collapses. As we stand, eroded by salt and tide, the horizon can be reclaimed, autonomy rediscovered. In the Empty Quarter, there is plenty of room for new stories to be born, plenty of space to let myself be an Essex man again.

David Southwell

a.

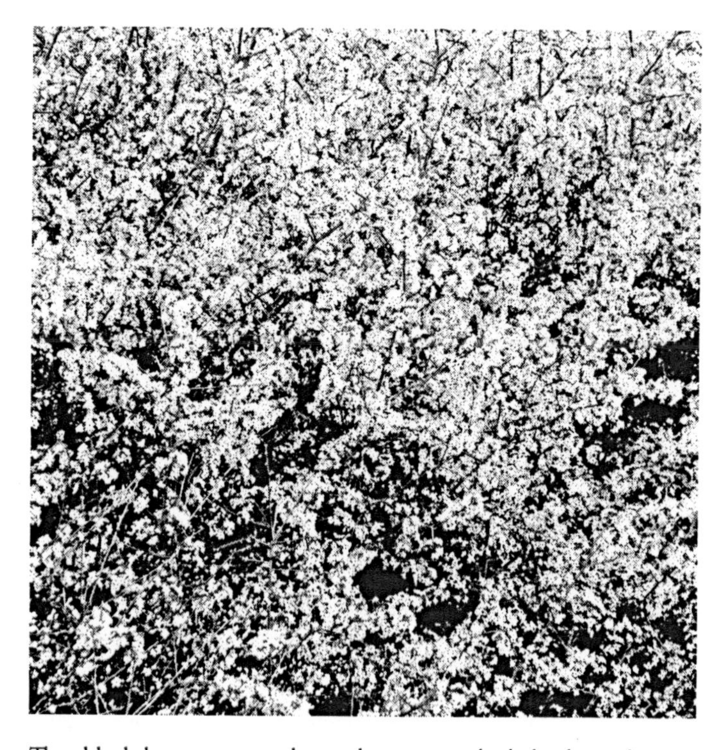

The blackthorn, near where the waters had broken the sea wall, had flowered earlier than usual. D____ wondered what it meant for the autumn's harvest of sloes and recalled the name of Juliana Berners, a fourteenth-century nun from St Albans, whose name was recorded by Wynkyn de Worde as Dame Julyans Bernes. Berners had written in her *Treatyse of Fishing with an Angle* how the 'sloe-thorn worm' makes for excellent fishing bait.

A Lazy Wind

"That's what we call a lazy wind, boy. It dun't go round yer, that goo straight through yer."

It's a rare year when it doesn't arrive to ruin the fun. From early springtime right up until late May, the mean north-easterly wind may come lashing down like a cane onto the weathered old buttock of the East Anglian coast. Even though the ripening sun viewed from indoors may appear warm in mid-April, step outside and there's that wind. Like a pinching resentful old crone, with her bony hand on your scrawny neck, she croaks at you, "I in't quite finished with you yet, Boy."

Delusional metropolitans, striding proprietorially around Dunwich and Aldeburgh in their stockman coats and broad-brimmed hats may fancy that by buying property here, they've somehow bought into some new Arcadia that will bolster their jaded souls. With the North Sea wind flicking at their ears, however, making their children grizzle as it scythes over Aldeburgh beach, they discover exactly what the natives have known for generations: East Anglia is a much tougher place in the cold months than it is during the golden section of the summer. The up-side of it is that the sharp spring light in those broad canvas skies so beloved of artists is also here.

East Anglia, flatter, drier and less-populated the farther

north you travel in the region, is a strange kettle of coconuts. Tragic bores and pedants still write letters to the regional newspapers, putting the case for declassé Essex not to be included in East Anglia. Large chunks of Essex, however, especially the north of the county, remain very much in East Anglia. Everything north of Maldon and east of Chelmsford, is firmly East Anglian. Strictly speaking, Southend, a good thirty miles from London, should also be included. For there in the far southeast are those same fertile tracts of flat farmland and reclaimed marsh that are the signature dish of the region. Until recently, too, much of Essex still retained vestiges of its old accent old countrywomen here used to greet their grandchildren with: "Well! Hevn't yew grow-en?" The pronunciation of 'growen' from the old Essex dialect, would have been recognised by the same East Saxons who gave Essex her name.

As you enter the county of Essex by road, the three notched, scimitar-like swords which you'll see on our county road signs, are called seaxes. A seax, pronounced 'shax', was a Saxon sword. The heraldic seaxes on the signs represent grain: the corn, barley and wheat that have always grown well on our farmland. Essex was once the breadbasket of London. For centuries our grain fed the metropolis, whilst our hay fed their horses. The hay, in fact, was shipped down the coast in great hay barges, which then returned laden with horse-dung and soiled straw from London's stables. The dung was chucked onto the farmland

and later, ploughed back in. Essex sent London its natural riches while the capital sent back its horseshit. Over a century later, culturally at least, some might say that not much has changed.

Essex, the UK's eighth largest county, with its third largest coastline, remains almost seventy per cent rural. To the surprise and possible chagrin of certain media types, Essex is rather more than the unappetising commuter-strip to which certain travel guide referred a few years ago. To the concerned classes of New Millennial London, Essex is a place of chavs, frontier driving techniques, the smell of old villainy and housing estates that look as if Triang had designed them. The poet John Betjeman famously described Essex as a place of sweet, uneventful countryside that was mirrored in ponds and often seen through gates.

The county, however, has always been regarded as 'common' – even though it possessed no fewer great houses and estates than its posher neighbours, Suffolk and Hertfordshire. Essex has always been on drinking terms with East London: both as a weekend love-nest and as a fishing and shooting destination. The two places are old kissing cousins. This is possibly because it was Essex where those Medieval cockney horse-traders originated. Even if the county is not exactly the same East Anglia as that of the middle-class caravanserais of Aldeburgh, Southwold, Holt or Holkam Bay, it's always been about the same in fishing and farming terms.

Interestingly, until the beginning of the thirteenth century, much of Essex, north from Forest Gate almost to Colchester, consisted of the Great Essex Forest. "They were woodland people," the author Ronald Blythe once told me when I asked him about our forebears. The traditional weatherboard house-building style is still common in the county today. It was exported by seventeenth-century English colonists to New England, where it's known as 'clapboard'.

A further East Anglian export to America at that time was witchcraft. Norfolk, Suffolk and Essex were once known as 'The Witching Counties'. People restoring old houses in the region, even nowadays, will still occasionally discover mummified cats in chimney breasts, bits of jewellery, old buried witch bottles and other strange ephemera intended to ward off evil spirits. Of the three East Anglian counties, however, it is Essex, sly, sharp-eyed and perennially up-for-it, that we'll now examine more closely.

Colchester, for instance, which in late medieval times, was one of England's largest and most prosperous towns, seems always to have had some sort of a chip on its shoulder. Like a queen deposed, Colchester must pay fealty to what many regard as her plainer sister, Chelmsford, the county town of Essex, thirty miles to the south. Noble Chelmsford, which Charles Dickens, for seemingly no reason, hated, suffered something of a 'make-under' at the hands of mid 20th-century town planners. The county town (actually a city), has a lot going for it. With an understated Georgian grandeur at its centre, it also possesses a good market, nice parks and pleasant suburbs. Talk to local taxi drivers, some of whom were born and bred here, and they will speak affectionately of the city. It was here, in the early 20th century, in a shed in nearby Writtle, that Guiglielmo Marconi invented radio. Chelmsford was also, round about the time of the Peasants' Revolt, for a very short period, the capital city of England.

Colchester may always have been, in its own way, damned ground. For it was here, circa AD60 that Boadicea burned the cakes – and pretty much everything else. The legend on the road signs greeting visitors proclaim Colchester as Britain's Oldest Recorded Town – a boast so tenuous as to veer into pathos. They may as well add, 'Honestly, we probably are!' As a piece of tourist PR this is municipal loser-mentality at its defensive finest. Contrast it with those straightforward signs that greet visitors arriving in Norwich: 'Welcome to Norwich – a fine city.'

Colchester, however, actually deserves more than it awards itself. The town is sitting on a far more legitimate claim to fame than its coy signs imply. For Colchester, in Roman Times, was actually Britain's first city and ought to say so. Those signs should read: 'Welcome to Colchester – Britain's First City. D'you want some?' That they do not do so is typical of successive borough councils' low-octane faffing.

It is true and commendable that we British celebrate our defeats with more enthusiasm than we do our victories.

For example we say 'Dunkirk Spirit' rather than 'Waterloo Attitude'. To celebrate the tribal sacking of our first city however – surely the 9/11 of its day – is wearing the hairshirt and leaving all the pins in it. Boadicea's vengeful Iceni savages came down on the occupants of the *colonia* mercilessly. They looted, burned and murdered, leaving no house unlevelled and taking no prisoners. Often celebrated by the misguided and the un-remedicated as part of Our Island Heritage, the episode was highly inglorious. Philip Crummy, Colchester's distinguished archaeologist, has compared the Celtic mob's destruction of the city to ethnic cleansing. The event was described by Winston Churchill as the most horrible episode in our island's history.

The event has left an ineradicable stain on the town. The second-worst event in Colchester's history, which occurred almost 1,600 years later, was the English Civil War Siege of Colchester in the summer of 1648. Here, the stubborn Royalist citizens of Colchester held out for eleven weeks, eventually being forced to eat their cats, dogs, and horses, rather than acknowledge that they were on a losing ticket. This type of hopeless obduracy is woven through the town's historical plait like a tattered and bloody ribbon. As we move on, we discover that Colchester, at least so far as suffrage was concerned, was noted by an early nineteenth-century observer as having had a distinguished place in the annals of controversy and corruption.

This is to say, that even when the few who now had the vote were able to exercise it, they either stayed away because of intimidation, or they voted for the Squire, because their forefathers had always done so – yet another thickhead rural tradition. Occasionally, the put-upon farmworkers reared up, and burnt a barn or two before being subdued by the militia and hanged. But that's about it. Welcome to East Anglia. A further interesting fact not often mentioned about Colchester is that during the early 1970s it had more mental hospitals within its environs than practically anywhere else in the country. I'm not reading anything into this of course, but I felt it my bounden duty to mention it.

As a young man, upon re-settling in the town, having spent my dissolute teen years in London, I was surprised to find many of my youthful contemporaries were rather negative in attitude. If there could have been a single phrase that summed up the local attitude it might have been "It wun't come ter no good, will ut?" It seemed hard to get artistic projects up and running. Nor, during the early 1970s when I returned to the town, was there much in the way of nightlife. Most of the town's venues had been closed down because, so the locals said, 'of the squaddies'. This was not entirely true. The townspeople themselves, many of them being of military lineage, were no strangers to the art of the roughhouse and readily engaged in punch-ups with alacrity, experience and skill. The borough councillors, in those days, were iron-clad old aldermen and women, who seemed to know their charges rather well and blocked any overtures from what they perceived as the 'permissive society'. For instance, all attempts during the early 1970s to stage any sort of a free pop concert in Castle Park were repelled firmly. At weekends, therefore, well into the 1980s, the town's nightlife was on life-support, if not actually stone-dead by midnight. This may have been more of a boon than some of us at that time realised.

Matters were slow to change but eventually they did. Young Colchester fought for what it saw as its right to party. The net result was that three decades later, in the small hours of weekend nights, the town's urinous, gum-splattered, kebab-strewn streets are thronged with young damsels and knights who now have the freedom to fight, screw like alleycats and drink themselves to early-onset diabetes. Exactly how much fun can Boadicea's bastard children have? While there's a profit to be made the jury's still out, as we say. There remain no shimmering nightspots in Colchester – only places where people become staggering drunk whilst endeavouring to attempt some clumsy type of love match. More usually they end up injuring each other. Colchester's 'night economy' – how I love that spin – is a classic example of a provincial town serving itself badly.

In recent years, when Colchester finally got its new arts gallery – the beleaguered and widely-disliked Firstsite – people were protesting before it was even built. It was as if a horde of hooded medieval peasants with burning brands had besieged the castle on the hill before the much-feared new occupant – in this case modern art – had even moved in. The punters got an art gallery, when what they'd actually wanted was a bus station. A fine difference between clever and wrong, we giggle, hysterically.

It would be unfair, however, to blame the council or indeed any local politicians for this state of affairs. 'People are people,' as the 1980s Essex electropop band Depeche Mode so acutely observed back in 1981. Besides, you can only piss with the pintle you've got, can't you?

Colchester's problem is that it is haunted by its own ghastly psychogeography. It is as if the very stones of the ancient town are so indelibly stained with ancient blood, misery and shame, that its collective psyche will simply not allow it to believe in itself. As a consequence, nothing here, it seems, can ever come to any good.

And yet I love the place. Because I can and often do walk around the town centre, on soft grey summer days. It is on such days that I'll sometimes glimpse, through the fog of recent ruination, the old Medieval core of the place. For centuries Colchester was a buzzing market town, a well-watered place on a green hill, with pleasant gardens, orchards and eight handsome parish churches within its much-patched walls. Many of the people who throng the town's careworn High Street nowadays walk around as if they were sleepwalking. If they could pause, just for a few minutes and then look up and around, they might see, as I sometimes do: the ghosts of a once-great theatre town, a home of engineering, agriculture, cloth manufacture, thriving small businesses, education, art and much else. Colchester was and still is at heart, a great little East Anglian town. The old girl, as I've already said, deserves much better.

Hidden (rather too well-hidden) within the town are 500 years worth of Medieval riches. These occluded centuries are akin to great unlistened-to songs on the town's historical jukebox. On constant rotation airplay are the bloody boring Roman occupation or the bloody repetitious English Civil War. Surely these two eras are respectively, the 'Dancing Queen' and 'Mustang Sally' of East Anglian history? Look, they're great, but I'm sick of hearing them.

Sweet architecturally, but currently regarded as unsexy, Colchester also possesses beautiful little suburban streets which are tucked away under its fustian overskirts. Ireton, Honywood, and Inglis Roads are fine, if typically unsung examples of late Victorian and early Edwardian streets. The area known as Newtown also has lovely streets crowded shoulder-to-shoulder with modest pleasant houses. In the early nineteenth century the Newtown area consisted of fields that became a garrison of tents and huts, housing thousands of soldiers hurriedly recruited for a Napoleonic invasion which never came. When the borough purchased the land back from the military a few decades later, Newtown was the result.

If Roman Colchester, at the far western limit of their empire, had been intended as a flagship city – a centre of commerce as well as a colonia – then the Romans bet on the wrong horse. Camulodunum, with its silty little river, was never destined to grow as prosperous as the far better-situated Londinium, then a wooden mercantile town, sixty miles southwest.

Colchester, though, has always looked less to London than east to the North Sea and the near continent, or north, towards its neighbouring East Anglian counties. An insular people? Possibly. Or maybe they were just happy where they were. I spoke a few years ago to an old Essex farmer and his wife, then in their seventies. They'd never left the UK. Their passport forms, they said, lay on the table in anther room where they'd been for ages, as yet unfilled-in. In the next breath, the couple spoke with moving affection of holidays taken decades earlier on the Norfolk coast. It came as no surprise to me that before the age of package holidays, many rural East Anglians took their holidays elsewhere in East Anglia. Quiet, unfathomable East Anglia with it wide skies and long dry autumns. Yet, still, each springtime, that mocking north-easterly wind, with no topography to impede it, flails down on it, all the way from the Russian Steppes. Then, despite the strengthening sunshine, the wind may set in for weeks at a time making men curse and turn up their collars. And, still, I stay.

Martin Newell

The Stars Shout Back

where else? for this marker -
withie staithe buoy pole
and at dead of midnight hour -
breeze that rose chill on the point -
where the old barge lay berthed
sunken encrusted teeth still ghostly
the story familiar
to all the inhabitants of the
never-to-be named hamlet
pretty huddle of houses
before the land runs out
down to the river, under the
hegemony of water , of
pools spits mudflats
one into the other turning, dissembling
saltiest estuarine / silted berths /
graveyards / where sloops ketches dinghies barges
turn on the tide
hard to imagine water
that was mud
become water
stealing back at the diktat of
moon-pull
emptying and filling, filling
emptying
as hard as to
fix life in the second it drains away

Wendy Mulford

Broad Memory

Curving about the spinning lighthouse,
Its silent cry unheeded,
Caught in the spiralling, windy robes
Of these cliffs; these breathing relics
Of an icier age when oceans marched
In stately progress beneath frozen waves.
Now these cliffs with regal assurance
Stand in defence 'gainst the late icy sea,
All melted now; ungoverned,
Impassioned, dark and devilish mass,
Each wave arising with hornlike prongs.
The cliffs still stand, and though crumbling here,
Though misshapen there, the cliffs still stand;
And over their backs, like a fateless fleck,
Through time and space was I flung.

*

It is a plain folly to deny that history moves in the mists of Norfolk, within those clouds that arise from the sea and engulf the land. Known by the neighbours of the North Sea as a 'haar', from the ancient Norse for hoary or grey, these fogs endure for days; they move in ponderous drifts and are so dense that at times one's horizon is no more than thirty feet away. The haar can be extremely localised, perhaps isolating a single village, and must be traversed with caution lest unforeseen nightmares emerge from the vagueness. As dangerous as the Norfolk haar might be, it is within these mists, which exist between the wide marshlands and cliffs, that the spectres of bygone days are preserved.

Our travels begin where all my journeys end, in the fishing town of Cromer, which bravely faces the iron sea. She is a strange sloping town forming an 'L' shape from the four pinnacles of the church tower to the fantastic limb of the pier stretching out beyond the coast. The town and the sea coexist with relative ease, though this has not always the case. Indeed, at one time Cromer was far removed from the abyss and relatively inland, for beneath the frowning arch of the horizon, beneath the swelling waves, lies the memory of Cromer's older brother, the town of Shipden.

It was a cold Medieval night, as the Angelus rang out over the rising gale, imploring the townsfolk to prayer, when a devilish storm was riding out at sea. It lashed the charging waves with its lightening whip and roared with malevolent glee. Terrified by the hollow crash of air against the cliffs, not a single man, woman nor child dared answer the Church's call for fear of being struck down without mercy, and so the village hid in terror. But the storm was too cruel to accept their submission. The galloping waves smashed into the weak shield of the cliff; rain and hail, like stones from a sling, were hurled against the earth; the wind tore trees and gorse up out from the ground; and the jetties and houses were swept away as the angelus continued to ring out over the chaos. The next day, Cromer awoke to a sky of remorseful pink hanging over the sea's flat and mournful expanse, like a satin cloth covering the tomb of Shipden.

Five centuries later, in 1888, the steamer Victoria was travelling en route from Cromer to Yarmouth when it struck an unknown object and rapidly began to take on water. The local fisherman rushed to rescue the passengers as the ship was consumed by the sea. When it was discovered that the vessel had collided with a church steeple rising above the waves, Shipden emerged from the mists of history and tales rapidly began to circulate.

But the lost town had long since been a present reality for the people of Cromer before the Victoria disaster: on frozen nights when the sea strikes out at the cliffs, a toll can be heard resounding under the storm; a sorrowful chime, again and again, like an Angelus bell calling the fearful to prayer.

*

Although Shipden continues to haunt the coast, Cromer now dominates the land. Nestled between the tall whitewashed lighthouse on the east cliffs (the area fondly known as 'Poppyland'), and the distant Beeston Bump to the west, Cromer embraces the sea with one arm and holds fast to the earth with the other. As a testament to this resistance, the church of St Peter and St Paul looms over the town as a solid mass of flint, forbearance and faith. Its tower, the tallest of any church in Norfolk, gazes far over the sea with Peter, the fisher apostle, who anxiously guards his descendants at sea.

As the coast bends around to the west, past Sheringham and Weybourne, the brilliant cliffs begin to diminish towards Holkham, as does the boundary between the earth and ocean. Distance becomes indistinguishable; the land slips into the sea; fog sweeps over the flats as swift as thought and just as deadly. From above, with the pink-footed and Brent geese, with the larks and pipits, one can view the hypnotic swirls of the marshes, spinning their routes through the centuries; the yellow shoals twist into shallow blue at the mouth of the River Glaven, contrasted suddenly with the rich velvet green of the undergrowth.

This obscure stretch of Norfolk, wavering between our world and the next, neither one nor the other, is guarded by lonely spirits and an ancient malevolence: the sands, dry one instant and flooded the next, clutch the ankles of the unwary; the winding marshes lead straying minds farther and farther from the known path; and for untold centuries the heavy pad, pad of Black Shuck has stalked the innocent traveller.

*

Must I recount the legend of the Shuck? If we speak of the devil will he not appear? Within the haar, the road of reason disappears as doubtful shadows become hideous realities in the growing red glare of Black Shuck's monstrous eyes. Even here, in the golden light of day, I can see him pounding towards me over the deserted sands of Holkham beach. Those terrible eyes burning with their unknown fire and no scrub or bracken to conceal myself behind.

The wild beach is merciless. The tide races in beneath my feet, softening the sand. It drags me down with every frantic step, as with every second the Shuck races closer. Claws rip the sand beneath them and those eyes tell of Odin's wars, of Lucifer's hatred, of ancient evil, pure and unbound.

The tales say that as the Shuck draws near, the hellhound's merciless stare can kill. Do I turn? Pad, pad, pad. So close, splashing in the shallows. What is he doing? Pad, pad. But Black Shuck is gone. He needs no nourishment but terror. We, natives of the earth, are conquered by an empire of fear that will not end.

One man to be ruled by this fear was Sir Arthur Conan Doyle. He heard tell of the hellhound whilst holidaying in Cromer Hall, wherein lives the muse of Baskerville: the hall was used as a model for the Dartmoor house. Conan Doyle fell under the spell of Black Shuck and sought to destroy the hound with logic. But is the Baskerville's curse an accurate depiction of the hound? The East Anglian Black Shuck strikes without bias, he serves no man, he is beyond reason. And Black Shuck truly exists, perhaps not in the world but in the elemental recesses of our minds.

The moment you fear venturing outdoors on a moonless night, or cannot define a menacing shape in the distance, or dread turning around to see what shadow approaches, know that it is the echoing pad, pad of Norfolk's Black Shuck pounding through time for you.

*

Do not suppose we always live in fear on this stretch of coast. The sea can crash as loudly as she likes, monstrous dogs can prowl along the beach, but the townsfolk of Cromer continue their simple life. Like the crab for which the town is perhaps most famous, Cromer's cliffs are encased with a hard shell. Only terrible storms such as those of 2013 – in which the mighty boom of waves is like a giant's fist, pounding down fortress gates – can reduce Cromer's fanciful summer palaces and quaint beach huts to matchsticks. Such are the cold realities of the sea beside which Cromer must exist.

But she does exist. Although the coast falls away about her, Cromer stands. The village of Overstrand to the east diminishes almost annually as the sea erodes her fragile cliffs. So too on her west flank the land rapidly disappears. It was here that in 1992, along the cliffs of West Runton, the fossilised remains of a steppe mammoth was discovered; the skeleton had endured for almost six hundred thousand years. It would be tactless to say 'so too does Cromer endure', but the metaphor holds some truth. The town seems to resist the full-blown effects of change. When the railways came, through the annual hordes of tourists, even with the arrival of the internet, some essence of Cromer remains unaltered.

In this way she represents the obscure and insular character of Norfolk, which is noticeable even in comparison to the rest of East Anglia. Indeed, it is an unwritten rule that to be 'local' a family must be a resident for fourteen consecutive years, so it is quite possible for a child born and bred in a town to be considered foreign. The Davies, the Smith and the Jones families still dominate the crab trade and fill the suits of the lifeboat men as they have done for decades, and the traditional order is still maintained.

For a young man attempting to escape the world of youth, which disappears underfoot like an eroding spit, the routine of life in Cromer is unbearable. From the annual carnival in summer; the 'lights-up' ceremony in Advent; the mad rush into the sea on Boxing Day; and the New Year's fireworks over the pier, to the daily rut of existence when the fishermen sail out to empty their crab cages; the tea rooms throw open their doors; and old ladies stop in the street to chatter aimlessly at one another, with their ridiculous, overburdened trolleys – all these once cherished memories become splenetic trials to be endured every day, week, month, year.

But without these habits Cromer would fade into a more terrible obscurity. She would be unidentifiable in a herd of cloned towns. Her streets would be unremarkable and insincere, her vista would lose its integrity, and she would become crowded with farsighted fools who refuse to see the path winding before them and dream instead of a motorway emerging from the horizon. Having lived so long on the border of the unknown Cromer advances with caution, one step at a time, in the glacial manner which formed her; however slow or simple this must seem, it is a safe and certain march.

*

Indeed, Cromer is the hard gem on the crown of Norfolk and she reflects many of the county's characteristics. Further inland, however, some of these traits change their manner, perhaps as the threat of the sea diminishes and the advantages of fluidity can be safely observed.

From between Mundesley on the coast and the interior town of North Walsham, the Pastons arose from impoverished obscurity to become a family renowned for their wealth. In the wake of the Black Death these peasants invested in property and in each other. They married above their station and ambition drove them to London. Eventually they became the principle beneficiaries of Sir John Fastolff's will, the knight who would be the inspiration for William Shakespeare's John Falstaff.

The Pastons were fluid, self-assured and aggressive, many characteristics that seem foreign to Norfolk. But elsewhere, in the county's literary past, a figure with similar traits emerges in an old and irritable pilgrim who served his master, if not honestly then at least with caution. Wily and feared, Geoffrey Chaucer's Reeve, 'From Norfolk, near a place called Balderswell', prefigures the Pastons' guile almost exactly. He dominates his superior through finance and cunning, growing rich enough to terrorise those beneath him.

The Pastons and the Reeve represent that mercantile class which eroded the Medieval aristocracy and emerged to build hard, almost impenetrable shells about them. In doing so they became the new aristocrats and would spread their values of fulfilling ambition through financial transactions far and wide, values that would be their downfall.

*

The same tides that threw the Pastons into the upper classes are ever present in the memory of Norfolk. The new merchants and the old aristocrats who survived the social upheaval built noble houses for themselves, like glass palaces floating on the flat landscapes of the county. Felbrigg, Blickling and Oxburgh, taken over by the National Trust; Holkham, proud and independent; Houghton, Mannington and Wolterton all thrown up by the Walpole family as symbols of their indomitable wealth and power.

These monuments to aristocratic magnificence will always be fragile in Norfolk, as the floods of 1953 demonstrated.

Swelling through the noble Broads, where live the dappled bitterns with their booming call, the sea raced inland, bursting through the reeds and cascading over the fields. Once secure towns vanished beneath the expanse of sea, and only the red roof tiles above the swell indicated that this area was once fit for human habitation.

Despite this severe warning from nature, the hardy, almost relentless people of Norfolk continued to challenge the authority of the sea. Now you can walk safely across the Broads, almost level with the water. On solid ground you can progress through the reedy veils and the ever shifting world of water.

*

Following this twisting route, along this path which challenges convention at every turn, we wind our way to the heart of Norfolk and the fine city of Norwich. It is a city of merchants and martyrs, with a history delicately woven from the reeds of the Broads and the wool from the vast pastures.

In the middle ages the traffic of this trade flowed across the county, through East Anglia, passing the Dutch Quarter of Colchester, thence to the rest of the country and beyond. Indeed, Norwich forged strong connections overseas with the Low Countries. The foreign weavers and craftsmen escaped religious persecution to settle in Norwich and consequently revitalised the East Anglian industry.

Throughout the city there are countless monuments to the vibrant trade of one of England's first internationally inclined counties.

But the city grew not solely on the back of commerce or under fear of oppression, as the forbidding cube of Norwich Castle, the image of glaring cruelty, might suggest. As the first merchants grew wealthier they built churches for the city, and records show that Norwich boasted fifty-seven churches within the her walls, one for every Sunday of the year. Only thirty-one of these remain, in addition to the two mighty cathedrals, the neo-gothic Catholic cathedral and the ancient Norman cathedral.

Within the former there stands a shrine to Our Lady of Walsingham, another jewel in the misty past of Norfolk. Back on the northern coast, fearless in the realm of Black Shuck, stands the Slipper Chapel, just beyond the miniscule town of Great Walsingham. The monarchs of northern Europe would make a pilgrimage to this site soon after their enthronement, and the village once rivalled Canterbury in its devotion. Today Great Walsingham is a site of universal prayer, and hopeful few, who escaped the secular world beyond the haar like Moses across the sea, still gather in their thousands to sing:

> Lady of Walsingham, Lady of England,
> Listen to a pilgrim's prayer,
> Come back, O Mary, come back to England,
> Back to your dowry, this island so fair.

*

Norfolk never sought isolation as her remoteness might suggest. When London raced to dominate the country, Norfolk made little effort to compete and pursued a different course entirely. Whereas other lands followed the cosmopolitan fashions, Norfolk followed the obscure path of longevity. Mindful of the dangers of a real tide, Norfolk remembered the devastation and refused to be swept along by the man-made tides of change. Thus, by common reckoning, the county declined.

Yet Norfolk can still shock and astound, still make us feel more than any simulation. Suddenly, through the fogs of obscurity, ghosts walk next to us. Memory floods over us with savage brilliance, as Boudicca swept over the Romans. Norfolk retains that power to overwhelm, to consume what we might think is important but is not lasting, those terrible monuments we spend a lifetime to build but which, on the final day, will be submerged by the deep. Instead, Norfolk can help us to see those precious gems of truth we thought had been lost long since in the shadow of time. Upon these gems, which are worth defending, we can build a lasting shell that will not break. Although the coast erodes, and while towns disappear into the void, in Norfolk memory is broad, it is the last defence and it is very much alive.

Edmund Blakeney

b.

The old dock warehouses had recently been used as a location for the filming of a war movie. Down-river, another derelict shed had been daubed with a succession of political graffiti. The words 'smash patriarchy' had been erased and replaced with 'the tories don't care'. Shortly after the European elections this was redacted to read 'tories don't care'. By mid-summer the graffiti read 'Peace'. Beside it was painted a flower.

A Field Recording

Field recording is for me about capturing a sense of place with some authenticity. That doesn't mean that a field recording is literally a snapshot, but rather that it honestly conveys what it was like to be in a specific place at a specific time. To achieve that, the most important part of field recording is the act of listening. Spending time understanding the space, what it sounds like, and in particular what it feels like. So, for me anyway, it's more a sound portrait than an objective document.

I stumbled upon doing this, completely, through a combination of things. I grew up in a village in open farmland in central Essex. When my mum would pop out of the house to do whatever she had to do, I was left alone. I would go out into the garden, or put my face up against a window, and drink in what I perceived as silence but was actually a rich soundscape in which I was simply alone. It was actually rather terrifying being left alone like that, but exciting too, and I would start to attribute sounds to things that didn't emit sounds – in particular the remains of a tree that had been hit by lightning and the relocated chain home radar tower at the Marconi research centre on the horizon. That was probably influenced by the TV and films I had seen up to that point – *Dr Who*, weird Seventies children's programmes.

When I was about seven I stayed up and watched

Hitchcock's *Vertigo*. It had a really profound experience on me... the hazy, slow-paced scenes of driving around San Francisco, drifting around Mission Dolores with the Vaseline on the lens. I didn't understand any of it, but for whatever reason I was responsive to it. As a child with a tendency to daydream, it was useful, that strange sense of melancholy and softness.

In my late teens and early twenties I had a lot of time on my hands and a hugely open mind. I listened to a lot of ambient and drone music. Good ambient music creates a sense of the sublime and drone music tends to push towards the transcendental, so I tended to listen to the world in those terms.

I was aware field recording existed but I had dismissed it as consisting of rather worthy ethnographic recordings, to be honest. What limited soundmaking I'd done had been with synthesisers. In 1999, a musician friend recommended a magazine called *The Sound Projector*, and it started to challenge my view, although rather typically I didn't do much about it. Then in 2004 I was in These Records, a great little secret shop, sadly now closed, near The Imperial War Museum, with a cat and a paraffin heater, and the chap who ran it recommended I listen to Chris Watson's *Weather Report*. It blew me away. It made complete sense – and it made me think that I should perhaps be doing this.

It took a while for me to seriously get around to it. I bought more field recordings and picked out what I did and didn't like. So, a lot more listening. Then, in around

2007, really by chance, a friend told me he had a digital recorder he wanted to sell – he was a real equipment geek and after something better. We met in a pub, had a pint, and I handed over an envelope of cash. In return I got this fantastic looking thing with a fluffy windshield that looked a bit like Einstein.

Learning initially was by trial and error. Record, critique, change, try again. Naturally these days the internet is hugely helpful – I read interviews with field recordists, and learnt more about microphones and fieldcraft. I picked up some hundred-dollar microphones made by a US company called Microphone Madness – those made quite a difference.

In 2011, I went on the first of two residential courses with Chris Watson and another sound recordist, Jez riley French, run in Norfolk by a great organisation called Wildeye. These courses aren't technical, although I learned useful things and got to try a wide range of kit. They really focus on fieldcraft and building experience. Chris taught me how to record a wasp nest – you have to move in very slowly below and between the sentries that hover outside, and then you can place the microphones right in the mouth of the nest.

Equipment has become a lot more accessible in recent years – and that's down to the emergence of good consumer digital recorders. Twenty years ago you would have had a Nagra that would probably cost as much as a small car. I have an A-Kit and a B-Kit. The A-Kit is the original Sony PCM-D50 I bought in the pub, with a separate Sound Devices microphone amplifier. My pride and joy is my pair of Danish DPA omnidirectional microphones I've placed on a self-modified suspension inside a Zeppelin-style windshield, made by a British company called Rycote. They sound beautiful and open, and really capture the feeling of a place.

The B-Kit is probably the one I use more, as it's easily taken on walks and holidays. Sometimes I just tape it up in a tree and leave it there while I potter off. It's a great little Olympus LS series recorder and those Microphone Madness microphones. I rig the microphones on a coathanger to provide some stereo separation. I also have some nice contact microphones and hydrophones – underwater microphones – made by Jez riley French. The most useful piece of equipment I have is a headtorch, though.

The equipment isn't difficult to set up from a technical point of view – digital recorders have done away with the complexities of working with tape. Once you've set quality settings on a recorder (I record at 88.2kHz, 24 bit) it's fine to leave them be. You just need to know where to set recording levels for a given situation. But there's a knack to microphone placement that comes with experience. If wildlife is an element of your work, then you need to understand how it behaves, as that will dictate microphone placement. If I'm recording in woodland I look out for clearings – that tends to give you a good variety of birdsong. And if you're after specific species, then getting to know where you'll find them is obviously important. Recording nightingales and tawny owls, for example, is mostly about knowing where they can be found.

Sometimes you're going to have to get in amongst the birds – that's particularly true of waders. Inevitably you're going to frighten them off – so once you've placed the microphones it's then a matter of waiting twenty minutes or so for them to come back. Obviously, as with bird watching, there's an ethical dimension to this. I wouldn't intrude on a breeding site of a rare species.

Looking after the kit is really about keeping it clean and dry. You can get specialist bags that protect equipment from the elements but allow for rapid access – I definitely recommend something like that if you're taking it seriously. Moisture is the big enemy – you don't want to get your microphones soaked.

I'd done things like rain recordings for years, just out of the window of wherever I was living with a cheap dynamic microphone. I suppose I would count those as my first recordings. A couple of years ago I made a recording of the Bomb Ballistics building at Orford Ness. Technically it's not perfect, but it really gets a sense of the way the building is exposed to and responds to the wind. It's very intense, but also very beautiful – the way the building converts the brute force of the wind into something almost musical.

I like to record anywhere that sounds interesting – by interesting I mean that the sound tells you something about where you are. Generally I like marshland and other empty spaces… and if it's got an old, hulking, creaking building on it, then all the better. East Anglia is full of marshland

and other empty spaces. We're really fortunate with the amount of remote space we have. I live near a river, and in the winter and spring it's quite something – the melancholy of wading birds, and particularly the curlew. The ebb and flow of the tide, and sunrise and sunset – and the way the affect the birdlife – all contribute to a wonderful soundscape that feels very East Anglian.

Orford Ness is a place I love to return to – it feels like nowhere else on earth that I've been to. The closest to it I've experienced is Yukka Valley in the Mojave Desert, where you get that real sense of apartness. I also like the gentler sounds of closed-in streets in villages and towns, and I want to record more of that. Contact microphones on creaking timber-framed houses, swallows darting about, picked up by a pair of stereo omnidirectional microphones – that would do it. A cooling, enclosed village space on a summer evening in north Essex or Suffolk definitely has a very specific sound and ambience.

Just being out there is important. It's not all about the sound. The most exhilarating experience I had was when walking along a road at dawn near Whitwell Common in Norfolk and a barn owl swept straight over me, in complete silence. I just stood there, stunned – I could understand why they're so closely associated with sightings of ghosts. In some ways the actual act of recording is quite secondary, and if you come back without anything it's not necessarily a disappointment. Being out in the world, and the sense of being part of the landscape and respecting it. That can be enough in itself.

What I don't enjoy, and this can allow the gloom to descend on a field recording trip, is sound pollution. You get great sound events caused by man-made structures everywhere – rattling boatsheds and masts, droning wind turbines, vibrating fences – and the sound of soft conversation of an evening is great, although I don't record that for ethical reasons. All those are quite interesting and add to the sense of what somewhere feels like. Road noise is a real problem that can ruin a recording. When we're in a place, the brain can tune out the sound of things it doesn't particular want to hear, to a degree. But microphones don't discriminate in that way, and, interestingly, the brain can't tune out that noise during playback of a recording. So it becomes an enormous distraction. As more and more roads get built it's going to become a bigger problem. People seem to get really upset about visual pollution – the classics seem to be pylons and wind turbines, both of which I quite like – but are less bothered by noise pollution. And yet if you go to Dedham Vale on certain days, the traffic noise from the A12 is really quite bothersome.

I liken field recording to fishing, although that's based on a romantic idea of what fishing can be like, as I was always hopeless at it and hated it. But the waiting around for a moment with the recorder running – it's rather calming. And, of course, when you hear something that's wonderful, then it can be exhilarating. And, as with fishing, where you have to prepare your tackle, you have to prepare your kit. Make sure your cables are neatly wound, that your batteries are charged. Maybe I should start referring to my equipment as 'tackle'…

Mark Deal

The Medusa Steps

a gaggle of masts –
beware
Medusa strait

cloud shadows
cast on calm seas –
the pier punctures

a young boy
looks for sharks' teeth –
time on his side

Harwich herons
just an illusion –
a ship disappears

crag and clay
cake shifting shores –
fleeting lives pass

battalions
of spinning stars –
stud distant sands

the cliff edge's
uncertain horizon –

a tamarisk lip

on spiral steps –
an old man waits
for youth to ascend

stinking green
Medusa flowers –
snaking stairs rise

Tim Gardiner

A free-form haiku sequence written about the Naze Tower in Walton-on-the-Naze, ordered in sequence of descent from the viewing platform at the top to the ground floor, and with each haiku reflecting the view from the windows on the nine different floors.

A Remembered Landscape

It starts with the worn steps of a mounting block at a church in Bradwell and a mother's childhood; a remembered landscape from before the Second World War, on the Dengie peninsula, a remote tongue of land extruded into the North Sea, squeezed by the rivers Blackwater and Crouch with barely a mile of land between.

An area haunted by history but hunted today by those in search of the wild. My mother did not need to search. She roamed both on and off shore, from Sales Point to Stone; this was a place of solitude and discovery. In the 1930s, the Dengie was a land farmed but not tamed. A child could spend all day building dens, looking for lapwings and wandering unhindered in this Essex outpost.

Visiting now, sixty years since the war ended, there is no trace of my family's beach hut. But some things still remain: the steps of the mounting block that so fascinated my mother, indented with years of use.

*

It was a November day with sun so bright it could have been our lost summer. We stopped at Bradwell-on-Sea, an Essex village of weather-boarded houses, pink washed cottages with dormer windows and a church perched paternally over it all. Following the lime avenue down from the porch,

I found the worn steps of the mounting block, the focus of my mother's childhood memory. It seems a small and insignificant feature from which to launch a discovery of the Dengie peninsula. But it is a reminder; a reminder of the effect of time on memory, on materials, on the land.

I came to the Dengie peninsula guided by photos and stories from my mother. I also followed the trail of the author Robert Macfarlane, who was in pursuit of migrating birds and the wild country described by John Baker in his book *The Peregrine*.

It was the coincidence of these writers' travels to the place of my mother's childhood that prompted this autumnal visit. I too find myself searching; looking for lost childhoods, looking for memories. It feels strange to stand beside the mounting block that for sixty years has been part of a remembered landscape. My mother's childhood was wild and free, an uninhibited and unstructured relationship with place that bred an unfailing desire for wilderness. Who had shaped this place and in whose footsteps would I follow as I crossed the peninsula?

*

A sense of place is influenced not only by geography but also by the imprint of those who lived there and the perceptions of those who visit. Since the Stone Age, people have moved through this coastal area. Some have left no trace, some have left their memory in place names or occasional artefacts dug from the soil and others have left buildings, fashioned landscapes and written accounts of their time here. I wanted to explore the make-up of this land, its geology, history, economy and natural history.

*

It is the geological and glacial history that provides the beginning of the story. The most severe spell of glacial cold brought the ice sheet south as far as Essex. The Dengie, as a result, is a mixture of alluvial soils, London clay and sands and gravels.

Looking east across the North Sea, it is difficult to imagine that around 9,000 years ago this peninsula was far inland. As the glaciers retreated, rising sea levels pushed back the coastline until about 3,000 years ago when the Dengie, and its embracing rivers, the Blackwater and Crouch, more closely resembled today's outline.

For a true perspective, one should approach the area by sea, navigating in through the maze of buoys along the Blackwater, half way between St Peter's Chapel at Sales Point and the Nass Beacon to the north. Beating up river, a small boat can slip into Bradwell Creek or anchor south of Osea Island as no doubt the Danes did many centuries ago. It is in a boat that one can sense the rhythm, the power and the fickleness of the sea.

This is a salt kingdom, accessed from the water and shape-shifting over centuries between sea and land. The relationship is central to an understanding of the Dengie. Perhaps this gives it its wildness. It is a transitory, insecure place where generations must have lived in fear of invasion by both men and sea. It is a landscape of loss – loss of land to the sea, loss of homes to invaders, loss of nature to civilisation.

*

In 1210, a law was passed requiring landowners to pay for sea defences. Since then, periodic combinations of wind and high tides have caused severe flooding. The solution has been to keep building higher walls. Maintaining adequate defences has to be a joint effort since a breach at one point can inundate the land of neighbours. Lack of funds was a problem in the nineteenth century and it is again today, when other options are being tried, including the deliberate realignment of the sea walls to create areas of marsh which absorb flood tides.

After the war, new housing was built on low lying ground and people moved in, probably unaware of the potential for another event such as Black Monday, the devastating flood of 1897. When the 1953 flood came, populations were vulnerable and the loss of life and harrowing tales of survival are still bitterly recalled.

*

The sea is not the only invader against which successive

generations have prepared defences. The once extensive Essex forest was a forbidding and perilous barrier to travellers over land, so the peninsula would have been accessed more readily from off shore. It is from here that Dengie's history comes – raiders, missionaries, mariners and smugglers.

My mother has a 1949 travelogue in the Vision of England series. The author of the Essex volume, Phoebe Fenwick Gaye, tunes into the landscape by reaching back to the origins of this kingdom of the East Saxons. Starting her journey in Maldon, she observes how the Forest of Essex once enclosed Maldon like a horseshoe, making of it a great place for defence. Yet the river Blackwater runs towards it like a spear; taking cover on the way behind Osea and Northey islands, and striking forward into the little town's heart; a great place for attack.

The Romans built their fort at Othona as part of a coastal defence system against attacks from Germanic tribes. The Essex coast would see successive developments to protect against invaders, culminating in the pill-boxes and airfields of the Second World War.

After the Romans departed, the area remained a pagan country until the arrival in 653 of a missionary bishop, St Cedd. Perhaps the Dengie is best known for the isolated chapel that he built within the ruined fort. It stands at the easterly point, keeping watch over marshes and mud. We are drawn towards it for its solitude and its survival. It features in travel books from before the Second World War as a romantic and forgotten relic.

*

I walk out to Sales Point, the northeastern tip of the peninsula. From here one can look across the Blackwater to Mersea Island or south across Dengie Flats to Foulness. It is all mud, marsh and shell bank. Walking round the peninsula's rippled edge, there is a sense of history unpeeling at each tide. A wartime pill box peeps out from beneath the sea wall across a narrow stretch of marsh buffering the coastline. The mud lies dappled with saltwater pools below the seaweed strewn tideline. Sitting on the white stretch of cockleshell beach, I can see the barges scuttled to protect the saltmarsh from erosion and the lines of weathered and frayed posts that could have been a jetty or the remains of the Saxon fish weir discovered by archaeologists.

*

The Flats that spread south from St Cedd's chapel are now reclaimed arable fields but once they were an important area for sheep. Recorded as early as the Domesday Survey, these coastal marshes or pastures were measured in terms of numbers of sheep. Not only did the flocks provide wool and meat, their milk was used to make cheese. The dairy heritage of these now vanished farms is reflected in place names such as 'wich' or 'wick'. For every ten pounds of cheese, a pound of salt was required. The Dengie marshes offered all that was needed for a thriving industry.

According to myth, a Roman commander based near Maldon, discovered salt production when his seawater bath was left bubbling as the fires burned underneath. He forgave his unfortunate slave when he realised this was a lucrative new occupation for him. Romans were paid in salt, giving us our word salary. It is difficult now to appreciate the historic importance of salt. Its ability to preserve food was invaluable.

*

From Sales Point southwards, the marshes stretch before me studded with the seedheads of sea aster and lavender and dotted with the red tints of samphire. Behind the wall, the marsh is tamed and drained, green with young winter wheat. Flocks of plover wheel inland and Brent geese betray their grazing place with their musical chatter.

I had passed a group of birdwatchers, clustered round an array of telescopes, keeping watch for merlin and peregrine. With strange juxtaposition, their base was by the empty three-roomed dwelling of the last of the Blackwater's punt gunners. Walter Linnett lived here in the shadow of the ruined Roman fort as his grandfather had before him. How different the world of the birdwatcher and the fowler.

To go back to the records of those wildfowling days is to discover the true nature of bird numbers in the years before the Second World War – geese passing across the sky in a formation perhaps a half-mile long and a quarter of a mile wide, and at low tide acres covered by widgeon, curlew and duck. The scale of the decline in those vast flocks of geese, ducks and waders is barely conceivable.

As a child of Norfolk, I am still mesmerised by the skeins of pink-foot that come off the saltings in the winter dawn or the gaggles of Brent geese that return to their saltmarsh at Holkham. But this Essex backwater, with its empty mudflats, must have been a humbling place to be; a landscape so full of wildfowl that the sky could blacken as it passed over.

There is now a sense of the thinning out of nature – wildlife I no longer see; the excitement of a flock of twenty finches, not the hundreds of my childhood; the abundance of birds that my mother remembers that are no longer part of our lives.

*

I have walked across the Dengie, and that process of walking, retracing paths, feeling the ground and smelling the salt wind, helps me reach back into the past.

The sun is beginning to drop behind the wooded upland of Baker's peregrine country and I must leave. I reflect on what I have learnt. Much has changed since my mother was here. The Second World War moulded the area for defence and a nuclear power station was later built on the airfield. The 1953 floods reinforced attitudes to coastal defence and left a legacy of respect and fear for the sea.

The agricultural intensification that prompted Baker's

concern for the future of nature has swept away many of the old mixed farms remembered by my mother; the community working together, gleaning the fields for spilt grain; milk deliveries by horse and indeed the loss of the horse as a working farm animal.

Dutch elm disease removed many of the majestic trees that defined the peninsula. The flocks of plover, widgeon and Brent geese, and redshank and curlew piping up from the marsh, are much diminished. The old wildfowlers and naturalists are gone and with them the intimate knowledge of nature where man seeks to become part of that world, albeit taking from it.

Some things remain: the villages, their names, their churches and their history. The Blackwater is salty enough for the Maldon Salt Company to maintain a successful brand. The creeks and inlets provide passage for boats, even if mostly leisure sailing, and the land and sea yield up a rich harvest.

The Dengie is still wild. It is a remote, open place in a constant shift with the sea. For anyone who is sensitive to the history, who can unpick the layers and recognise stories from the small clues surviving, this is still an enigmatic piece of country and a journey back through time; a landscape of all that has been and all who have been here.

Melinda Appleby

c.

There are only 90 living examples of Populus nigra ssp. Betulifolia, the black poplar, left along the Suffolk coast and fewer than 8,000 mature specimens across the UK. What tree we looked at here we did not know, but D_____ explained animatedly that the loss of floodplain woodlands over the last two centuries had directly contributed to the black poplar's decline. Later we spotted the first cowslips of the year.

Runways to the Past

The giant hangar doors have just opened to allow a small human figure to emerge blinking into the daylight. The audience too is slowly coming back to earth after a spin round the several Earths of Norse mythology, the violent crack of Thor's hammer still ringing in their ears.

Eastern Angles has just finished its final show of Ragnarok, the saga relaying of the doom of the Gods in which their battle with the giants ends up in annihilation for both. At the end of the evening performances, the Christ-like figure exits into darkness, but it's a matinée and outdoors is the one place you can't black out. Well, unless you unleash a nuclear winter, but we'll come back to that.

We are on the old Bentwaters airfield, just north of Woodbridge in that hinterland between the A12 and the North Sea. Bentwaters was built at the end of World War 2, but only came into use afterwards as the home of the United States Army Air Forces jets and tank busters, stationed there in response to the supposed Russian threat. It's a remarkable site, and our play, Ragnarok, which translates as Armageddon, took place barely a jeep's ride from the bunkers we now know held the nuclear bombs that could have heralded our own Cold War doom.

But the venue itself is also remarkable, since it is the hangar where the Americans tested their jet engines and, in an equally remarkable act of hubris, tried to reduce the deafening noise to a minimum by soundproofing the place. Or maybe it really was social concern – after all they re-directed their flights during the Aldeburgh Festival to avoid spoiling Benji's adagios and leave the interference to the rattling of the audience's jewellery. They clearly failed to limit the noise and locals still recall the tumultuous roar that nullified almost any activity when the engine testing was going on. But in that attempt they created a venue with the acoustic of a recording studio and a tunnel to give any actor an entrance to die for. Oh yes, and the irony is they called it the Hush House.

Standing on East Anglia's largest Cold War site, watching the onion lorries buzz back and forth and the comings and goings of various business unit inhabitants, is like watching history on the move. One set of structures is suddenly re-colonised and transformed into neutral territory. The old hangars perch like crows across a bleak landscape cut through by a runway that seems to stretch into infinity. You can only experience it by traversing it and momentarily glimpsing the haze that hangs over its mid point. It's as if the tarmac momentarily obeys the arc of the earth. After all this is the runway now reputed to be the longest in Europe: it was specially extended so that should the Shuttle have to land on this continent there would be a welcome in the flatlands of Suffolk. And once landed, since it wasn't designed to take off, that shuttle could still be at Bentwaters. If only!

As our audience disperses, slightly overwhelmed by the physical nature of the piece they have just witnessed, but perhaps more fearful of getting lost on the site, it's time to dig down and ask the questions that roost around this ominous space. For the other remarkable thing about Bentwaters is that under the runway is supposed to lie the site of the palace of the Wuffings, the tribe that ruled the kingdom of the East Angles for nearly 400 years and whose most noble princes are buried up the road at Sutton Hoo. Now you see how one play can conjure so many roots and routes of significance.

The Angles were attracted by one of this region's unique features, the gorgeous estuaries that lace our shore, the great vulvas of our coastline that faces Europe. For we have no real rivers, nothing like the Tyne or Tweed or Severn. Each of this region's estuaries peters out into something little more than a big stream, which, with constant dredging, might allow a snail-like barge to crawl towards some market town to exchange London horse dung for straw. This physical geography also means that we have no coast road. Instead, the A12 meanders its way round the heads of each watery or muddy lagoon, depending on the state of the tide. This means any visitor has to turn off and travel at least five miles to find the coast; picking their way through gorse, pine and sandy soil. Hence the special secluded nature of those coastal habitations.

But those estuaries were the means by which first the Angles, in stately new-farmer fashion, and then the Vikings, in slightly more aggressive manner, found their foothold in this area. The Angles were clearly homesteaders and rooted themselves almost by default. In fact, in the summer of 2014 my family and I drove through the Anglo-Saxon heartlands of Schleswig Holstein and south Denmark and suddenly realised why the Danes liked East Anglia so much – it was just like home, except they now had spanking new barns and no traffic. You could see why they stayed here, if not why they left.

Is it too long a stretch to compare the experiences of current inhabitants of East Anglia with our Angles ancestors? Eastern Angles thinks not. Eighth in the East, a separate project I helped set up, is exploring the effect on local landscapes of the arrival of the American Eighth Air Force. Working on this, it dawned on me that until the Friendly Invasion, as it was termed, East Anglia had hardly seen the machines of war since Boudicca or the Battle of Maldon. When the Anglo-Saxons settled it was as peaceful farmers, the Normans harried the north, and the Civil War found little to fight over in the relatively un-castellated east. Apart from a few rick-burnings, broken threshing machines and occasional skirmishes with smugglers, the region was a pretty quiet posting for the average dragoon. The *Victoria County History* says that even during the Wars of the Roses all East Anglia heard was the quiet click of the trowel as its churches were rebuilt.

Should I be surprised that having spent years packing village halls to the rafters with our shows, we are getting people to leave the security of their community venues and venture somewhere alien like an old airfield to watch a show like Ragnarok? Maybe not. After all, within our cosy rural world we still name Tuesday and Thursday after Tyr and hammer-wielding Thor, the Norse gods of war.

Ivan Cutting

Easter Parade
(Chelmsford Cathedral)

The flowers in the cathedral grounds
Fluttered like the banners and buntings
Of an easter parade, only groundbound
Rather than against the celestial sky.

Passing, days later, they were gone,
Their beds now rich brown circles
Of soil, perfectly geometrical,
Like the crop circles of artists or aliens.

So clear, so simple, what better
Silent sermon on resurrection.

Tim Cunningham

Drift

Bookended by once-great ports at either end – both Great Yarmouth and King's Lynn were once grand enough to justify their qualifier – the Norfolk coast curves smoothly east to west along the top of England's beer belly. Pare it away from the rest of East Anglia and you are left with a 'D' on its back, a hoop of liminal geography. Or a crescent moon, fallen to Earth – a moonstruck landscape of moon-governed topography. The sea accounts for everything here, one way or another, and, as is often said, time and tide wait for no man.

This is the east and so no fractal West Country coastline here, no rocky cliffs, few convoluted bays and inlets. What you get here is a smooth curve of sand, pebble and mud, the boundaries blurred as sea melds with sky and beaches dissolve to saltwater: sky blue – sea-green – ochre. Or grey – ochre – grey, depending on the season's mood – a minimalist tricolour to represent a kingdom of ozone, salt and sand. The visual clichés are there for the taking: big-sky beaches, fishing boats glowing red on dun mud creeks, seals that flop on the sand like obese sunbathers, dunes spiked with marram grass, groynes that slope away to sea like mussel-studded garden fences. Such photogenic components are the North Norfolk coast's brand icons (there is no South Norfolk coast, of course – the 'north folk' (Norfolk) are separated from the 'south folk' (Suffolk) by a mere river).

It begins in the east – that is, if a coast can 'begin' at all – at Hopton-on-Sea between the ports of Lowestoft, England's most easterly point, and Great Yarmouth. Hopton, home to Potters, a family-oriented holiday resort (its mantra: 'a village not a camp'), belongs to the area known as Lothingland, a tract of land hemmed in by the River Waveney and Breydon Water that was part of Suffolk until it fell into Yarmouth's (and Norfolk's) orbit in 1974.

Great Yarmouth, a seafaring town that grew up on an isthmus between the North Sea and the River Yare, has been obliged to reinvent itself several times over. Once a thriving port (Daniel Defoe describes it as 'an ancient town... for wealth, trade and advantage of its situation, infinitely superior to Norwich'), the town has been through incarnations as a naval port, herring fishing centre, holiday resort and North Sea Oil base before arriving at its current uncertain state. Despite multitasking modernity, the apparatus of Yarmouth's holiday heyday remains more or less intact: a promenade with two piers, a winter gardens pavilion (re-homed after a failed tenure at Torquay), several amusement arcades and a Sea Life centre. The Britannia Pier retains its end of the pier theatre too – Jim Davidson territory, his natural habitat; or was until he refused to play the town in 2006, describing it as being full of overweight people in flip-flops. Now he's back, all seemingly forgiven.

South of the centre, in a half-empty industrial estate, close to where the Yare reaches the sea, stands a monument. The 'real Nelson's Column' some call it, this is where Britannia

– olive branch in one hand, trident in the other – perches aloft a neoclassical column above six caryatids. Constructed in the early 1800s to celebrate Nelson's hammering of the Spanish and French navies, the question remains: why does Britannia look inland rather than out to sea? Is it because she gazes with maternal protection towards Nelson's birthplace at Burnham Thorpe on the other side of Norfolk?

Closer to the centre along South Quay are further reminders of Yarmouth's nautical heritage in the form of 'rows' – narrow lanes of tiny cottages, once home to fishermen – but the streets that lie between the river and Marine Parade exude a more alienated, down-at-heel ambience. Here, alongside tattoo studios and low-rent charity outlets, are shop windows filled with jars of pickled vegetables and fluorescent-lit cafés that show Brazilian soap operas on TV. The ciphers in this part of town are inscrutable to most Yarmouth natives as signs alternate between curly-tailed Portuguese and the car-crash of consonants that is Polish.

Holiday parks and serried ranks of metal boxes – caravans not shipping containers – grace Yarmouth's northern reaches as it approaches Caister-on-Sea, almost a suburb, not that many Caister folk would agree. "Caister men never turn back" is the motto of the plucky lifeboat crew here, and they don't – there's even a Never Turn Back pub in the town. The sea is a different matter though and throwbacks sometimes appear. A former seafront hotel, The Manor House, long claimed by the waves and virtually vanished from local memory, made a phoenix-like comeback in 2013 when its foundations were revealed by a winter storm that had scoured millions of tons of sand from the beach. Previous to this, the hotel had been last seen in 1948 when, having been abandoned during World War 2, it finally crumbled into the waves. The revenant building – just bricks and piping after all these years – serves as a reminder of the fragility of human settlement on this capricious shoreline.

Further north, at the village of Winterton-on-Sea, Defoe, visiting in 1722, records that most village houses seemed to be constructed out of wrecked ships' timber. He may well have been right, as an entire sailing fleet perished off the coast here in 1692. There are those who insist that a wrecker's mentality still persists in the village gene pool and an undercurrent of lawlessness still pervades the area. But it is a more innocent cargo that attracts locals to the shoreline here these days. The beaches and dunes north of the village are a favoured spot for seals during the winter pupping season – cuddly objects of curiosity for strolling families and dog-walkers who come here for a sniff of brine during the Christmas holiday period.

For an even more tangible sense of the raw power of the sea, follow the arc of the coast north to Happisburgh. Happisburgh, pronounced not 'happy' but 'haze', has a red-and-white banded lighthouse that is visible for miles in the flat relief of northeast Norfolk, a necessary beacon on this wrecking coast. It is at Happisburgh where the effect of coastal erosion on human life can be seen at its most dramatic, especially when a winter storm arrives from the northeast. It is here that the cliffs can be seen visibly crumbling onto the beach below, leaving those properties that stand foolhardily near the cliff edge ever closer to oblivion. The lighthouse, constructed a little way inland within a nest of houses, still has a few decades to go before it buckles as a result of the inexorable progress of time and tide. Only in Happisburgh can you see this coast's inevitable fate written quite so plainly. Beach Road, an eastbound lane wide enough to have no-parking double-yellow lines terminates dramatically at a cliff edge, its sheered tarmac surface and hardcore foundation exposed like rock strata. Beach Road has now become Beach Leap: blind-faith sat nav devotees beware.

The unseen vector of nature's force here is longshore drift. Such is the potency of its shape-shifting power that the landscape reads like a textbook diagram – an arrowed flow offshore thrusting north along the coastline before rounding the curve to the west. Along the northeast Norfolk coast its effect is one of savage erosion: scouring sand from beaches, chipping remorselessly away at cliffs, undermining the properties of those foolhardy enough to build close to the sea. But once past Cromer, having turned the corner, its role morphs to that of depositional, dropping its accumulated load to create sandbanks and spits, silting up harbours and estuaries in the process. Kick over a sandcastle in Caister-on-Sea and a year later you might find the same grains of sand stuck between your toes at Holkham beach.

The drift is inexorable, although there are those who think that more could be done to stop nature in its tracks. It was ever thus: King Cnut, no imaginary monarch but a real king who had sovereignty over much of England, Norway and Denmark in the early eleventh century was, apocryphally at least, a would-be tide-stopper. Northeast Norfolk still has a number of latter-day Cnuts, and groynes, concrete sea walls, sloping revetments, gabions, cliff drains, boreholes, shingle banks and even massive stone blocks imported from the north of England (euphemistically referred to as 'rock armour') have all been employed in attempts to decelerate the inevitable decay. Despite all this, 'managed retreat' is now the watchword, an expression that has just the slightest hint of a Jonesy-esque 'don't panic!' about it.

Happisburgh has other claims to fame beside dramatic erosion, as it was in this immediate area that some of Europe's earliest hominids once walked. As recently as the last ice age a land bridge extended across to the European mainland and in theory it was possible to walk all the way from England to Vladivostok given time and decent footwear (although neither commodity was abundant back then). In 2010, flints tools were found on Happisburgh beach that were thought to be anything up to 950,000 years old, the oldest artefacts of this kind in all northwest Europe. Such antiquity would indicate that the tool-makers were most probably Homo antecessor or 'Pioneer Man', whose bones have been previously found in Spain. In 2013 a set of fossilised footprints was also discovered, the earliest found outside Africa. If these early hominids were present here nearly 1 million years ago then there would have been plenty of game for them to hunt – mammoths, sabre-toothed tigers, hyenas and the like. It would have been cold though, with chillier winters than today – all of which begs the question (and simultaneously suggests the answer): did they control fire?

Sea Palling, Happisburgh, Mundesley, Overstrand . . . the coast curves smoothly westwards until it reaches its tipping point at Cromer, a seaside town with all the necessary ingredients – pier, lifeboat station, beach, tall-towered flint church; even a small fishing industry that plucks deliciously sweet crabs from the nearby sea floor. Cromer's pier points due north like a compass needle, nothing to spoil the view all the way to the North Pole. Far out to sea, beyond the horizon, lies Dogger Bank, a sandbank in shallow, fish-rich water (its canine tag a familiar character in the hypnotic poem that is the BBC Radio *Shipping Forecast*: '...Dogger, Fisher, German Bight...'). Back in the Mesolithic, when early man was flaking flints and chasing mammoths on Happisburgh beach, this same territory would have been the Dogger Hills, an upland area of Doggerland, a vast area of land, now submerged, that once connected England with Denmark. Trawlers have dragged up the remains of mammoth and lion from the seabed here, along with the odd prehistoric tool and weapons. Gazing north from the pier towards the horizon, it seems odd to think that hunters once strode where crabs now scuttle.

Behind the town lies a wooded ridge, Norfolk's highest ground, the tide-mark of a retreating glacier of ten millennia ago. The ridge stretches west behind Cromer's genteel neighbours: Runton – East and West – and Sheringham, its old fishing rival. A little way to the west of here is a marked transition, a cultural sea-change, a boundary crossed. It is around this point on the coast where the dynamics change and the geomorphology shifts from erosional to depositional, and dunes and sandy beaches are replaced by meandering creeks, mudflats and reedbeds. It is somewhere around this point too that another transition takes place, one that is less easy to measure than that of mere shifting sand. Heading west from Sheringham, a cultural divide slowly becomes apparent, although it is hard to say where its exact boundary is. If a north-south divide bisects England between the Wash and the Bristol Channel, placing proximate settlements on either side of an imagined cultural and economic partition, then is it too much of a conceit to imagine a similar sort of east-west division splitting the Norfolk coastline into two?

East of this tipping point we have a Norfolk full of indigenous folk alongside the occasional displaced Cockney and blow-in from the Midlands or the North. West of here though, natives are altogether more scarce (locals cannot afford the inflated house prices) and blow-ins are largely replaced by weekenders and second homers. This is yacht-owning territory, a highfalutin world where the fish and chips of northeast Norfolk have been replaced by pan-fried sea bass and crushed new potatoes. Substitute square plates for Styrofoam containers, jus for gravy and slow-roasted pork belly for burgers. The villages here, although picture-perfect, are a little unreal: the realm of *Country Life* property porn – a *Daily Telegraph* heartland where middle-aged men sport bright corduroy trousers and a little too much nostril hair while their wives dream of Benedict Cumberbatch.

The epicentre of this kingdom – rural Norfolk re-imagined for a metropolitan elite – has to be Burnham Market, not quite on the coast itself but a short, eight-iron putt away. Burnham Market: 'Chelsea–on-Sea', 'Burnham Mark-up' – the jokes are old but true. Like a stockbroker belt commuter village, occupation of the red-brick cottages is transient – a weekend dash up from The Smoke for a bit of sailing, golf or a stroll on the beach. A pilgrimage best performed on expensive German wheels, a members-only ley line traces the way north from London and the Home Counties. Ironically, it is this same part of the coast that is touted by the style magazines as 'hidden', 'undiscovered' or any other of the contemporary memes of metropolitan desire. Such is the difference from the sterile environment in which they work that visitors hardly notice that, decanted to the coast, they are almost entirely surrounded by their own type and class, paying prices that mimic London levels. None of this really matters: they are relaxing in 'darkest Norfolk' and 'it's good to get away'.

Of course, northwest Norfolk is not simply a matter of gastro pubs and sky-high property prices. It is also a dreamy landscape of marshes, mudflats, creeks and shingle banks; a scenic backdrop for extraordinary wildlife – seals that bob in the sea like doe-eyed Labradors and more wading birds than you can shake a Zeiss spotting scope at. Indeed, Cley-next-the-Sea actually deserves its overused soubriquet of 'Mecca for birdwatchers' as any vagrant bird blown haplessly across the sea to make landfall here will be thoroughly scrutinised and noted for its lack of local credentials before it hardly has a chance to dip its bill in the mud. The same might be said for would-be house hunters in some of the more exclusive villages along this stretch – even a bulging bank account may be insufficient without the right cut of jib.

Spits and tidal creeks, huge sandy beaches and dunes at Holkham and Holme, the flat top of Norfolk between Cromer and Holme-next-the-Sea obediently follows a line just short of 53°N as it leads into the sunset. Norfolk's Ultima Thule is at Scolt Head Island, which isn't an island at all but another spit, its nesting terns and wintering geese on loan from the Arctic. Just beyond Holme, the coast bends south once more as it confronts The Wash. Holme, which boasts both a splendid bathing beach and a nature reserve is a place where sunbathers and birders vie for attention – although there is plenty of room for both. A natural turning point, it comes as no surprise that this is a locus of sacred geography, a fact reinforced by the Bronze Age timber henge that was discovered here a few years ago. Quickly dubbed 'Seahenge', the awkward question of what to do with this chance discovery soon developed into a four-way squabble between locals, archaeologists, naturalists and didgeridooblowing New Agers. Seahenge may have just been an inverted tree stump surrounded by posts but the site was clearly 'of ritualistic significance' as archaeologists are wont to say. Its carefully preserved timbers, now stripped of all mystery, can be seen in the King's Lynn Museum.

Beyond Holme, the coast veers sharply south towards Hunstanton and King's Lynn. This is Norfolk's sunset coast, west-facing across the Wash towards Lincolnshire, a contradiction for a county so far east. The Wash is a vast rectangular repository of mud, salt and lugworm, another food-rich sanctuary for wintering wildfowl. On a clear day Boston Stump, the vertiginous tower of the town's St Botolph's Church, can be just about discerned but usually there's a haze through which distant, disembodied turbines are seen rotating on the horizon, the far shore beyond sight. The corner of the coast having been turned, things start to get rather more humdrum and workaday. After the rarefied atmosphere of the attractive yet aloof villages of the northwest coast, Hunstanton ('Sunny Hunny'), a cheerful resort with a hint of McGill postcard saucy charm, comes almost as a relief. South of here lie caravan sites and more beaches and bird-rich mudflats before the Great Ouse River and King's Lynn, the coast's western bookend, is reached.

A mirror image of Great Yarmouth in some respects, King's Lynn is older, with narrow medieval streets and historic Hanseatic League connections. Once this was a whaling centre that ranged as far as Greenland and Canada, but ships sail from here no more, fish (or whales) are no longer landed and the voices on the street are more likely to be those of East European migrants than wobble-legged sailors. But on Purfleet Dock the town's former maritime tradition is still remembered by way of a tricorn-sporting statue of Captain George Vancouver, a native son of the town. Two Norfolk seaports, east and west – Yarmouth and Lynn; two Norfolk seafarers – Horatio Nelson and George Vancouver: the curve of the coast is complete.

Laurence Mitchell

Shingle Street to Felixstowe

Stand on the beach at Felixstowe and stare across the mouth of the River Deben – to the whale back sand bars, to the vast, glorious folly of Bawdsey Manor. A spray of exotic tree tops rises unkempt above the perfect oriental cupolas, their china blue, eggshell virdigris glorious even against the cloudy skies. To the east the red crag cliffs fall to the grey German Sea; to the west sit the matchbox houses of the quay. At the gloaming time head south to Landguard Common. Creep in the shadows of the cranes, those hideous monster herons leaning poised above the waters. There stands an acropolis of steel: modern temple for the Port workers, lit in the glowing glare of artificial light. On Langer Park, strange, stepped statues rise from the beach in dusk-deceiving shadows – sacrificial sites it might seem, but no – just the bare butts of gun emplacements, mere mementos to the fear of foreign feet invading – like those stoic stone shells, the towers of Martello; the pill boxes peering out to sea. Invasion haunts these Suffolk shores: Remember the Dutch at Cottage Point, whisper the ghosts of Landguard Fort. Four hundred years is nothing to a land which seeps dinosaur bones from its soils, deposits sharks' teeth on the beach at East Lane.

James Canton

His Winter View

Lighting the cigarette, he imagined the ploughed field at the end of the garden, the one that he gazed at whilst sitting at his kitchen table. He thought about how unchanged the field was from last month, or how the slowness of its seasonal changes made each minute alteration seem almost deliberate, as if this portion of the visible was, in some sense, perfectly camouflaged, or was only revealed in the movements of its camouflage adjusting: as if the familiar, striped, patch of sky and earth, the gap in the bordering hedgerow that lined the field's close side, this threadbare, skeletal, meshing of twigs and branches opposite his windows, framed a presence that generally evaded his sensory capacities. Or perhaps it was during his breakfast, in those stretches of stirring his tea and spreading his toast – perhaps here he merely stared for longer and with deliberate intensity at this one patch of earth and sky than at any other, and so caught solo glimpses of a general quality amassed in the outlying landscape, one whose manifestations he normally failed to register in the urgency and hurry of each day.

Vaughan dragged on the cigarette, and breathed out at a steep angle, towards the clouds. These, like streaked paint smeared on a distant, high ceiling, were more a textural change in the sky than marked by a distinct colour or outline. Then he thought about how the field had been last year and the winter before. Any differences were as scarcely noticeable as the aging of his face over this time. It was as if slowness was ingrained and entrenched here, as if the folding over of rotting leaves had been allowed to set the pace and mark the hours. He thought how unimaginable any changes to this landscape were. They were as inconceivable as the final mask of old age on the face of a companion that we love when we are young – an adored face that is of those icons or totems of a youth that is left behind, irretrievable, as we age – those that are mourned for, silently; or one of the icons or totems that the mad and old, the shattered old, seem to be searching for in their interminable wandering of the streets, their ceaseless ramblings; the kind of icons or totems flickering in the mind of an aging man when alone and smoking, standing behind a house whose frame is stretched into tautness by the pressure of its emptiness. One of these suspended over Vaughan each night as his chest inflated and lowered in nocturnal breathing. A home that is silent of other voices; those that call to him by shouting down from upstairs, ones asking familiar questions each day in the same room at the same time, voices he knows so well that he can predict what they will ask in a moment, just from the tone, from the angle of the head and the quiver in the iris before the first triggering word is uttered.

Vaughan felt the cold begin to penetrate and raised the fingertips of his left hand to his cheek: it was clammy, firm like refrigerated meat, as if the lowering temperature was hardening and contracting his flesh. He sniffed and took a shorter drag on the cigarette, then, as he exhaled, he thought about Catherine's and Greg's spare front-door key on his kitchen table. This soothed him and he raised himself up on tiptoes and down again, repeating this movement a handful of times, trying to warm his feet. He considered walking through the garden to the field. He wondered if the darkness would be abated in the field, if a distant grouping of light, some street-lighting or the lights of the city, may have lessened the darkness, this darkness that he felt to be a covering folded over and over and over; as if the bare exposure and open distances of the field had allowed the fragile light, the endangered glow, to gather and collect; as if the darkness was an emission from the trees and structures, from their ordinary, ladder-length, summits; a coiling vapour that spiralled high to circle in layers; one dense enough to press the faint electric light to its edges, dispersing it to gather over fields or forests or oceans, in the sliding and receding of this gas of pure dark.

Vaughan walked forward, stepping off the decking and onto the lawn. Then he remembered how, at this time of year, the mud in the field froze into hard, compact lumps: the pesticide and nitrogen fertiliser-laced mud with its slight resemblance to soil, the mud that always seemed thicker and stickier than was natural, that coagulated into solid, dense discoloured clods with their tinges of yellow and grey, their bristles of old wheat stalks. Vaughan thought how easily he could slip and twist, or even break an ankle, on this terrain of turned earth frozen into boulders.

He thought of the cold, unmoving plateau of mud of the field and the dredger-trawled sea bed. He thought of the marine, silt mud of the English Channel, or of the Irish Sea bed churned into lifelessness; of the haze and murk in the band of deep, sluggish water drifting like phantoms advancing over the flat, grey deposits; the mud compressed by the pressure of the heavy fathoms of saline water, the permanent weight. He thought of the cold down there, a static cold of tombs in winter, being disturbed by the silent thump and impact of the dredging tackle, its forward, mechanised jerk into motion and then dragging progress, rousing mud into turbulences like snow tumbling in an avalanche, these propulsive clouds born of friction; or of a passenger jet crashing, skidding and sliding, in a field, borne along relentlessly towards a transfixed observer.

In the mornings over breakfast, when he gazed at the field, birds were the only creatures ever visible, flocks of pigeons; or of crows or rooks, these flapping and cawing, battlefield, carrion birds, hopping from mound to mound on the just-tilled earth. He thought of the borders of this field, and the other nearby fields, linking them to the enduring impressions of ancient foundations of square structures; the archaeological marks, the brand of brick and stone, the dark dirt. As if the soil and the stones were the fine, centuries-sifted debris of a former age of progress; one that was almost departed, almost entirely lost, except for the sheer accumulation of its traces, the horizon vastness of its relics; the overall design, the coherent pattern, all of these only visible from altitude, from the aerial or satellite positions.

Lander Hawes

d.

We had travelled across the fields in search of a red-crested pochard that had apparently taken to splashing in the quarry ponds. D_____ had a childhood fear of quarries and had until recently believed that south Suffolk and north Essex were full of them, whereas in fact there are only a handful. The corrugated iron shed, once a common sight in the British countryside, also made her feel strangely uneasy.

Digging

"Make the sign of the cross," the vicar instructs. He is dressed in a black wool cloak, fastened with a hook and eye clasp of silver metal; his appearance would not have been out of place, I think, a thousand years ago or more. It seems appropriate to the solemnity of the occasion and the sense that death gives time itself a disjointed, provisional feel. Grandma's ashes have travelled to the suburban municipal cemetery in Liverpool, to be scattered in the same plot as Grandad. I have made the trip to a distant, unfamiliar city, to coincide with a scattering of distant, unfamiliar local mourners. We are gathered in a horseshoe formation in front of Plot Eight, under a yew tree. The grass is slippery with leaves. Carrying the flowerpot-brown container, I lean clumsily forward in my pencil skirt and shake a thin layer of grey powder across the soil in two intersecting lines.

"There's a lot there," the vicar says as I hesitate. "People often don't realise how much there is."

So I carry on pouring, up and down the outline. There is no sound but the hushing of the ash as it piles up and up. Out of the corner of my eye, I catch sight of my sister's mouth in an enormous 'O'. The damp creeps through the thin soles of my unsuitable shoes.

There are prayers and words of committal. But I do not feel at ease in the environment; it strikes no chords.

I have never been back. I am not even sure I would know the name of the cemetery. My parents' premature deaths left a social and geographical chasm between me and my Grandma's generation, cutting me off from my roots.

*

According to *How to Read a Graveyard*, Peter Stanford's exploration of burial practices over the centuries, most graves are no longer visited after fifteen years. We are a more mobile society and one in which death is pushed out of the way of our daily lives. And yet we still feel the pull of the ancient dead. Twelve years after the interment of Grandma's ashes I visit Sutton Hoo. We may have deserted family memorials but this burial site of Anglo-Saxon kings is a popular place of pilgrimage.

It is early April and still unseasonably cold. The sun is struggling out; the grey sky is beginning to be striped with blue. The area around us is unassuming scrubland with clumps of gorse flowering garish yellow. The land rises gently to the east and, apart from the National Trust buildings and the occasional barn, there is little sign of human habitation. Yet there is something unnatural – in both its senses of uncanny and manmade – about the gentle mounds which undulate around us: from a distance, like static waves; closer, like the sea about to break above a breaching whale. Something is under there, something intentional, something concealed. Something in the land that we need to read.

This is what attracts me to places like Sutton Hoo: the need to read the signs; the possibilities for interpretation; the mystery that still remains even after extensive investigations. Looking at the landscape, I realise how my assumptions dictate what I expect to see and why the remoteness of the location surprises me. I grew up in a village where the dead were buried in the local churchyard; the ashes of my parents still share the consecrated space with the living, who pass them every Sunday on the treacherous, algae-ridden, flagged path. Where – high on this deserted heath – are the remains of any settlements? The answer is that they were never here. The Anglo-Saxons had a separate, assigned place for their deceased ancestors: remote, imbued with its own atmosphere. Sutton Hoo is a liminal place: a threshold between the living and the dead.

When the Anglo-Saxons arrived, following the withdrawal of the Romans, they came up the River Deben and settled on the fertile ground on the opposite bank. On a tour of the mounds, the steep gully can be seen where the present town of Woodbridge takes advantage of the same location. Soft beneath our feet is a carpet of moss and topsoil. Under that, explains our guide, is sandy, acidic soil, difficult to farm. Instead, the heath at Sutton Hoo became a burial ground for their Anglo-Saxon royal dead; perhaps those who were connected with the palace or mead hall at nearby Rendlesham.

As our guide leads us on to the burial ground, she

recounts the dramatic history of the 1939 excavations and of the redoubtable landowner Edith Pretty and her decision to investigate the mounds on her property. She contacted Ipswich Museum and a local amateur archaeologist and former tenant farmer, Basil Brown, was recommended to her. Not trained formally in archaeology, he was a man who was experienced in reading the land, the lie and the feel.

"He rolled up on his bike one morning." Our guide makes a cap-touching gesture. "And he said, 'Morning, Mrs Pret'y, what can I do for you?'" The investigations that followed led to the dramatic find of the ship burial under Mound One, a tale that combines the primitive excitement of the treasure hunt with a sub-plot of class tensions. The acidity of the soil had dissolved all organic material, but Brown was guided by the presence of iron rivets that had once held together the planks of the clinker-built hull. With the help of Mrs Pretty's gardener and gamekeeper, he painstakingly uncovered the sand-shadow of a vast longboat.

Once the burial chamber had been reached and its untouched state indicated a major find was imminent, professional experts took over. Charles Phillips took over the excavation (he is described as "one of 'those' Cambridge dons") while Brown was demoted to carrying on uncovering the hull of the ship, until Mrs Pretty stepped in to support Brown and assert her authority. Brown is now the one who is remembered.

"We have school trips here and all of them know about Basil Brown," says our guide. "Charles Phillips has entirely disappeared." There is evident satisfaction in the triumph over the collective memory of this local man of the land.

Up on Mound One, the wind is fierce. We clutch our hats. Anorak hoods billow like sails. My ears sing. On top, it is easier to take in the massive length of the ship that once lay beneath the mound – seventy feet, marked now with a wooden stake at each end. I can make out a ridge in the grass under which the prow of the boat once lay. It is as if it is rising out of the earth once more to make for the sea.

Burial in a boat symbolised the journey from the living to the dead. I wonder how the Anglo-Saxons saw that journey and what they thought they would reach when they got to the end. We don't really know their pre-Christian beliefs on life after death, although there may have been an idea similar to the Norse Valhalla, where warriors feasted in an eternal Great Hall. Christianity brought the hope of heaven but, in the early church, teachings on the liminal state between earthly and heavenly life were still being explored. Augustine and other Christian thinkers speculated on the nature of an intermediate state of purification and atonement for sin. Until the formal doctrine of purgatory was developed in the twelfth century, alternative landscapes were mooted amongst theologians, like explorers speculating about the gaps in their charts where the sea monsters were depicted.

A pervasive theme of Anglo-Saxon poetry is the experience of exile, and I wonder if the afterlife was seen in that light.

In 'The Seafarer', the poet is forced out from the warmth, protection and comradeship of the mead hall into the cold, unforgiving elements. He draws a nostalgic contrast between past comfort and the hardship and loneliness of his wanderings, accompanied only by the birds, symbols of his exile: 'Sometimes I made the song of the wild swan / My pleasure, or the gannet's call, the cries / Of curlews for the missing mirth of men.' The poem is not without a sense of keen spiritual exhilaration, but it also has an overriding heaviness: for the Anglo-Saxon poet, to be cut off from the human, social world, is a kind of death.

We have the words of these ancient, unknown poets; we also have, remarkably, the crumbling remains of the possessions they talked about – the shields, the drinking horns, the jewelled belts, from the digs at Sutton Hoo. To evoke the moment of the discovery of the burial hoard is to imagine the glinting of gold amongst the dulled and tarnished silver and bronze; the helmet in brittle fragments.

Mound One contained the largest and most magnificent collection of grave goods: plates and bowls made of precious metals, weapons, personal possessions and remains of clothing. The size and magnificence of the burial was probably a piece of propaganda to demonstrate the wealth and power of the royal dynasty, the Wuffinga. The mound itself was a clear message to strangers coming up the Deben, its prominent position a sign, saying, 'We're here; we're powerful; don't mess with us.'

The burial in Mound One, thought to be that of Raedwald,

high king of all the English regional kingdoms from Kent to Northumbria, took place at a time of religious transition. Converted to the incoming religion of Christianity at the court of the previous high king, Aethelbert of Kent, there is evidence that Raedwald may later have sought to keep the peace with both the old and new divinities. Bede, the early church historian, notes with disapproval that Raedwald built an altar at Rendlesham to both Christ and 'the devil' (presumably the Norse god Woden, from whom he claimed descent). Raedwald's wife, whose name is unknown to us, was resolutely pagan and resisted the new faith. Was she responsible for a final, grand, pagan spectacle for Raedwald's funeral rites, sending out a defiant religious statement with the splendour of the grave goods? Yet the move towards unfurnished graves that is associated with Christianity may not have been so much theological as practical. The new religion brought a new age of literacy and bureaucracy in its wake, with the potential for an early form of inheritance tax. This must have had an effect on what even the rich were willing to bury with their dead.

These days, we look upon the burial of the dead with objects for 'use' in the afterlife as an example of the naïvely literal nature of ancient beliefs on life after death, yet we still talk of the deceased as having 'left us', 'passed over' or 'passed on'. Death as a journey is a remarkably resilient image that both informs and is reinforced by physical experience. When I sat by my Grandma's side, after she had drawn her last breath, I felt her hand withdraw slightly as her muscles relaxed, as though I were letting go of a mooring rope.

One detail inconsistent with the pagan picture painted by the Mound One burial is the presence of two silver Christening spoons found amongst the grave goods, inscribed in Greek with the names 'Saul' and 'Paul' – the names, before and after conversion, of the missionary apostle. The spoons remain suggestive but inscrutable. Do they tell a tale of divided loyalties? We have so little data, so few physical objects from that period, that what we have can be made to bear a disproportionate weight of interpretation.

This is not only true of the distant past. Soon after my dad's death, which occurred after my mother's, my way of knowing him became a kind of archaeological enquiry. In the years to come, odd comments from friends and resurfacing memories would often disorientate. The day after Dad died, I stripped his deathbed. Although the body had already gone to the funeral director's chapel of rest, my actions felt ritualistic. To my surprise, as I pulled the sheets loose, my hand knocked against a hard object. Extracting it from the tangled folds, I found that it was a Bible. I had not seen it before, or known he possessed it. The story of how it came to be there is still mysterious to me.

Dad was agnostic in his beliefs, but was he reading the Bible as preparation for the unknown journey, the eternal wild of Bede's famous parable of the sparrow? This sparrow flies swiftly in through one door of the hall, and out through another. While he is inside, he is safe from the winter storms; but after a few moments of comfort, he vanishes from sight into the wintry world from which he came.

These words are placed by Bede in the mouth of a nobleman who is persuading King Edwin of Northumbria to accept Christianity. An individual's life is compared to the brief flight of the sparrow through the mead hall before disappearing into the darkness. This seventh-century view sees Christianity as attractive because of its claims to illuminate the unknown landscape of eternity in a way the pagan religion did not. The thought that Dad found the Bible a helpful map in his last days does comfort me, so I expect I would not readily relinquish this theory in favour of a possible alternative – that the book was left by a Christian visitor and Dad was too polite to refuse it. Perhaps we always bring our own agenda to our explorations of the past, and can never truly achieve an open mind.

*

Before I leave the tour of Sutton Hoo, I find an answer to a question that had been bothering me. Where were the ordinary people buried? In 2001, near the mounds, more modest remains were found – some burials and some cremations, perhaps predating the mounds, relating to a possible small farming community on the other side of the Deben. One man, probably a farmer, is buried with a warrior's spear, to lay emphasis on his role as protector of his community in death. I am touched by the way he has been given the props with which to rise to the occasion. The metaphorical transformation of this corroded iron point makes this ordinary farmer more of an Everyman figure; his spear a symbol of the ongoing interest of the dead in the world of the living, part of the landscape's shape and atmosphere. The ancestor-worship of primitive tribes now makes some kind of sense. We don't want to be held in thrall by the dead – but the idea that we can wash our hands of them, that we can just move on, in the way that contemporary culture suggests, cannot be right.

I walk back to the station. Back in the shelter of the Deben valley, I pause on the Wilford Bridge and look out over the estuary. The tide is out. On the bank, by the marina, a sturdy iron barge is grounded in the silt, pausing between transports of freight; next to it is a fibreglass motorboat with a collapsed cabin, growing fragile with lichen, evidently going nowhere. The mud is marked with a filigree of wader footprints, a pattern of radial spokes. Two curlew fly overhead; a redshank digs delicately for food on the exposed river bed. The mounds can no longer be seen from here, as woodland now hides them; the landscape of the past retreating from view. Here the National Trust is protecting and promoting the site, but all the time, elsewhere, clues to the past, the abandoned landscapes of the ancient dead are being built on, destroyed or washed away.

In one of my own poems, 'Archaeology', I compared the compulsion to seek for clues about my parents, following their deaths, to an excavation; as if the material world could give answers. How futile it is, and how necessary.

All are shards and scraps.
Gently, in places, I scrape the soil, and,
Where rough shapes appear, brush with soft hairs.
The eggshell arch of a forehead. A hand.

Elaine Ewart

The Lavender Bush Outside No. 19

(Hillside Road, Billericay)

All summer I passed them on the hill:
The satellite bees on a lavender bush
Bright with the winking of fairy lights,
Silent as Trappist monks, bonded
Like Amish neighbours building a barn.

Dressed in their swag-bag stripes,
They climbed in the shrub's open windows,
Burgled perfume, vampired the lilac-blue,
Their bee-line return pollinating
As if shaking dust from their heels.

Today, one lay in the shadow of the bush,
Dropped dead from its labours;
Not like a slave, more a windfall apple.
Undertaker ants polish the hearse.
They too have their template.

Tim Cunningham

The Chapel

After my father died in 1976, my mother wanted to buy me a place where I could live. I had been living an unsettled life on the dole, painting and writing.

We were sent details of the former Methodist Chapel in Westleton. It had lain empty for eight years, and was bare inside, with dry rot in the dado panelling. I learned that the congregation had dwindled and that latterly services had been held in the schoolroom at the back. The asking price was very low compared with what it would cost now, but other buyers had been put off by the lack of a garden.

I had been looking for a barn in the middle of nowhere, having lived happily in one some years before. This wasn't a barn, and it was in the middle of a village, but it seemed to offer possibilities that I hadn't foreseen: I could be secluded at the back, which was essential, but I would also be able to open the doors to the street and things would happen. It had a tranquility: it was a magical threshold.

After months of tortuous negotiations, I was able to move in and start making living spaces so I could be warm in winter. I had expected to be viewed as something of an outsider, but from the outset everyone I spoke to made me feel warmly welcome.

After two years, I started to put on art exhibitions, of my own and friends' work, the occasional sale being a bonus. Many of my own paintings had sexual themes. I was nervous as to what the response in the village might be if I showed these, so I broached the issue with several pillars of the community. They were blithely reassuring, so I went ahead: but there was a strong reaction, which led to my being politely asked to remove a few of the works.

I had been trying to be very respectful of people's thresholds, so was dismayed to have caused an upset, but happily it healed over quickly. There was a sequel, however, when I showed some of my drawings here a few years later. I heard from a friend, a retired bishop, that he had called on an elderly man in the village, whose daughter, a nun, was also visiting. The man was venting his fury about my drawings, although he had not seen them. The bishop and the nun, who had, stoutly defended me.

Some of the more edgy local teenagers and their mates took to hanging out in the Chapel, talking, testing limits, painting, playing guitar, and romping. I had welcomed and enjoyed their presence, but it reached a point where their demands were heavier than I could sustain, so I stayed closed through 1981 to reclaim my space.

During this time I became a passionate frequenter of second-hand bookshops, spending what little money I had in them. When the exhibitions continued, I also displayed some books from a local dealer to sell for him on commission.

In 1983 I was visited by the art dealer Victor Musgrave. Someone had suggested to him that my work might be of some interest to his Outsider Art Archive. In the event, while he thought that my art training showed through too much to interest him in my paintings, he expressed interest in the intense written daily records I had kept for years. And, before leaving, he asked if five hundred pounds would be any help to me. He explained that he was the advisor to a charity set up to help 'deserving artists'. After demurring briefly, I gratefully accepted and with the money was able to pay for driving lessons – and buy in the stock of books.

Business gradually grew. I came off the dole, started a family and the bookshelves began to crowd the walls until there was no room for exhibitions. I was employing helpers, particularly to help mind the shop while my children were here, and then all the time when I also had the Pinkneys Lane bookshop in Southwold from 2001 to 2003.

For about twenty years Chapel Books had evolved with little rationalisation amid a clutter of domestic junk: this was wonderfully polarising, putting off some people, and delighting others. Many were moved to say 'don't ever change', and, as I felt it was part of me, I had no intention of 'changing' it. But while focusing on the Southwold shop I inadvertently disconnected somewhat from the Chapel, so that, when my attention returned to it, I realised it now felt neglected, no longer vital. In order to reconnect with and revivify it, I had to work my way back into it by tackling the detritus. Rather than trying to recreate a semblance of how it had been, I tidied up. Twelve years later, people still remark on what they variously see as having been a great loss or a great improvement. There is now less ferment of chaos, but it is better for the books. And putting in floors for storage and sorting has been very satisfying.

When I started, no one knew me, and it was a problem to obtain books: now it is unusual for a day to go by without being offered a bag- or a car- or a house-full, most of which I have to turn down. Trade is generally seasonal: customers come from all over and online I sell round the world. I can no longer imagine how it all worked before the internet.

Now that my children have grown up I enjoy running the place mostly on my own again. While of course the local community is hugely important to me, the bookshop is determinedly non-proactive in connecting with it.

It still and always feels to me the natural and ideal place to be: a beautiful part of the world, my home at the back being a retreat, and the Chapel being an extension of my private space, into which people naturally come: an arena for interplay. Many people still seem to feel it has a benign vibe that touches them in some way, beyond the sum of the books. And their vibe rubs off on me.

Robert Jackson

Bateman's Tower

Brightlingsea, Essex, 1884

Agnes waits in her leaning tower for storms
and on calm nights dreams of lightning
flashes illuminating the glassy pentagon,
top floor of what is not a lighthouse.

Underneath, foundations were raised
using bound bundles of wood.
Her father has built it for her own
good, to live in pure fresh air.

The door is high and heavy, shaped like
those in church. She cannot pull it open
to see the curving shore, flatness of grass,
but the salty smell of fish floats up to her,

she hears gulls shrieking
above the harbour, muffled voices
from fishing boats as men set out for the day,
quietly because they know she is there.

At each rising tide her building
shifts, creaks as it inhales
brackish air, breathes freely,
moves to the perpendicular.

Her cheeks glow scarlet, blood flies
as she coughs; she is being consumed,
her lungs turning to white lace
inside her shrinking chest.

When the storm comes she commands
her weak body to stand by the glass,
burning eyes flashing over the creek,
blinking, blinking the boats home.

Thyrza Leyshon

Painting Place

The time I set out, the equipment I take, the clothes I wear – it largely depends on the conditions on any given day and, if I'm by the water, on the nature of the tides. The decision about when and where to go is more instinctive than planned and for me this is a deliberate part of the working process, to allow continually for the unexpected. The only constant is that the work will be made outside in the open and executed in one continuous sitting. Often this means working without a break for two or three hours at a time.

Sometimes I begin the day by walking along the water's edge in Landermere or when the tide is out by retracing new or familiar routes across the meandering tracks over the tidal marshes. When the morning tide is rising I might row further out into the maze of creeks and inlets, to find some hidden corner of the backwaters. This could be soon after sunrise when the light is clear and the stillness is broken only by the sound of birds, or, on cold winter mornings, when the silent landscape is shrouded in a sea mist. Or it could be late afternoon, when the wind drops and vivid reflections play on the water's surface, a time (often during the golden hour) when shadows throw the shapes of the land into relief or the low winter sun creates dark silhouettes in the silvery light. And occasionally I might continue on into the night, guided by the soft moonlight and working simply by feel and memory.

When I head out I carry only what is essential with me: a sheet of thick handmade paper taped onto a board and a shoulder bag with water and a box of materials, as well as some kind of waterproof and a plastic sheet, either for sitting on (where the ground is soft or wet) or for use as a makeshift windbreak, or for covering work in a sudden downpour. On colder days I use fingerless gloves to stop my hands freezing too quickly. At times, in an open boat or out on the marshes, I get very wet but that's just part of the elemental engagement I'm looking for. In Vermont last year for example I would often set out for the day in snow boots and mountain jacket with a roll of paper and specially cut lengths of plywood tied with improvised rope handles that could be carried from place to place along the icy river banks.

There isn't really a typical day, although at times I find myself concentrating on a particular patch of ground, a location that might be long familiar to me but which I want to revisit under new conditions as a way of extending the conversation between past and present, between what resides in memory and what emerges in the present moment.

Sometimes I work continuously over a period of days, rapidly making and remaking a series of smaller images, only some of which I will keep. At other times I will work on one large image from the beginning to the end of the day, recording the shifting weather and light as well as the constantly mutating shapes that rise and fall in the tidal waters. There is also a solitary oak tree by the water's edge that I return to at different times of the year, continually recording its passage through the seasons from the spare intricacy of its winter outlines to the unfurling growth of spring and the dense verdancy of summer.

Often I will work on smaller pieces at an old wooden table that faces out onto the creek in front of the King's Head in Landermere, or if it's going to be a larger piece I'll cut a two-metre length of paper and fix it to an old wooden door that lies on the ground. The paper is then saturated in rain or river water before being marked and stained with pens, crayons, coloured ink and gouache. Often I combine these with mud or other organic matter found on site, and in order to keep the image fluid and malleable I will then allow the rising tide to wash over and even submerge the picture surface during the working process. In this way I can continue to work without pause for many hours, allowing the various pigments to float, drip and run over an absorbent surface, before they eventually begin to settle and dry on the paper. Often the result is surprising and unpredictable, with earlier markings resurfacing through transparent overlays or delicately mapped out areas fading away beneath opaque washes. Only when the image has completely dried out, which can take some days (particularly if the atmosphere is damp), can I then see how the assorted natural and man made elements have combined and whether I feel it has succeeded or failed as a picture.

For me the specific locations are incidental, it's more to do with their proximity to water. The estuarine and coastal landscapes of East Anglia often seem on the verge of dissolution, of melting away into an empty expanse of sea and sky. Beyond the tideline they have an unfixed quality, marginal and uncultivated – a wilderness of reflecting light and shifting patterns. Robert Macfarlane describes in his essay *Silt* this soft bluish silvery haze that causes the elements to blend and interfuse – to produce a new country that is neither earth nor sea.

When I first saw the Blackwater estuary on a silent winter's day fifteen years ago, the glistening expanse of mud and silt reminded me of the desert. One of the islands in this luminous tidal realm – Osea Island – seemed to float like a mirage on the horizon. Only accessible at low water via an old Roman causeway, it was otherwise completely cut off, a self-contained parcel of space and time, and the sense I had that day (and the many that followed over a seven-year period) of being alternately connected and isolated was very appealing. The place moved to its own rhythm, a vessel of ancient history whose fragile lineaments were constantly being broken up and recomposed by the surrounding waters.

I stayed on the island for periods throughout the year, recording on paper its ever-changing liminal quality while enjoying (in contrast to the extended journeys across unfamiliar terrain which have often informed my painting process) the sense of sitting in one place and watching nature's myriad forms pass me by. And beneath the surface, there was the constant pull of the past, of glimpsing in the mud and creeks fragments of the island's history – old tracks, boat carcasses, shell banks and oyster beds – as well as those transient signs of more recent use, the remnants of a Victorian pier and empty concrete bunkers.

The layers of the past buried in the soft ground of the East Anglian coast have entered literature and my reading of *Great Expectations,* as well as WG Sebald's *The Rings of Saturn* and Roger Deakin's essays, have also played a part in my work. About eight years ago, when we left the island and moved further north along the Essex coastline to a location at the end of a rutted farm track that now sits precariously on the edge of Landermere creek in the Walton backwaters, I was fascinated to discover that Arthur Ransome had based his book *Secret Water* on the surrounding maze of islands, channels and inlets. Paul Gallico's *The Snow Goose* was also filmed here.

There is in these low lying landscapes a hidden quality, places of silence and occasional abandonment, where nature rises and falls, where things appear and disappear in the cycle of tides, and the passage of other lives drift to the sound of birds and waves – an often floating world where the mind slows down and reflects.

The elements are an essential part of the work, and with the work on paper done here in East Anglia it is the weather's unpredictability that guides the process, preventing the easy repetition of familiar motifs or any certain knowledge of the outcome. I can begin working on a clear day and suddenly what I'm seeing vanishes into a fog or rolling storm clouds. The shapes I'm drawing start to merge and dissolve while rain spatters and dapples the coloured surface, and sometimes washes it away entirely. In wintertime the northeasterly winds can make it hard to work at all, while on a dry summer's day I often have to work much faster, before the crayons I'm using become too soft or the pigments too dry, leaving the paper's surface frustratingly static and unresponsive.

But there have also been times when I've felt I'm wrestling with rather than responding to the weather. Making watercolour drawings in the dawn light on the Tibetan plateau was complicated by the water turning into ice on my brush, a problem I also encountered in Vermont when trying to wash the surface of a large picture in a mountain stream and then watching as icy particles formed all over it. In these extreme environments, snow can also fall rapidly, carpeting the ground where I'm working, and when it melts, as it did later on in the month I spent by the Gihon river, the snow and ice floods the landscape and tears away trees and vegetation from the banks. At the other extreme I've worked in arid desert locations where I've had to be very sparing with the water I'm carrying so there's enough left to drink as well as to mix paints. And when it finally ran out on one occasion I had to fall back on a can of Coke to finish the picture.

I was recently asked whether there is a complex, symbiotic, relationship of creativity within the process, where nature is shaping the work as much as I 'shape' nature by fixing it, however loosely, on paper or canvas. I think that's a good way of putting it. Explaining this relationship in another article I said that the final image belongs as much to the elements as the artist who began it. This applies particularly to the work on paper but relates equally to my paintings which, although much longer in gestation, are also a record of process and time. Some years ago I did a series of paintings based on a journey to the Himalayas where I wanted to represent the way the natural minerals and pigments, found locally in the earth and rocks, are used to paint man-made surfaces with vibrant symbolic colours and how, through the corrosive action of wind and water, they eventually dissolve back into the ground. If the paintings are a meditation on this process, often done from memory in the studio, the work on paper has a more immediate and visceral relationship to the natural world; they are both about, and shaped by, the place where they're made.

Perhaps this is best elucidated if I describe the way the process might begin: by registering marks, things that catch the eye – a passing bird, a blossom, a cloud, tracks in the mud, bits of flora and fauna. An accumulation of phenomena, both distant and close at hand, that creates a kind of equivalence, a response on a particular day to a place. It appears familiar but remains strange, a mutable scene that is never quite the same as the days blur and seasons shift, where streams alter their course, swelling and diminishing over time, and where mud flats that were previously sparkling black and silver are now softly carpeted in pale grass and wild flowers. What forms is a series of recorded moments, a diary of days composed of sequential memories (recalling the last time I was here) and sensory stimuli of the most immediate and fragile kind. It is a way of proceeding that is openly receptive, avoiding correction or revision while keeping the elements continually in play. The materials I use dictate this process, so a picture of the water is made with the water, the scattered marks and colours running in a way that directly mirrors the tidal flow that surrounds it or the rain that sweeps over it.

The writer Robert Macfarlane put it this way in a letter he sent a while ago:

'I might try to articulate what I find so unusual and compelling about the work: its localism, for a start. But also the hover between encryption and archetype (enigma and fabulous openness). As you hold on to a leaf, a shell, feather or pebble before returning it to its microcosmos, you learn to see not the names of things but the things themselves. Absolutely. We are both collectors, but not in the possessive sense of that word; quite the opposite. Surrenderers of sorts.'

A sense of place is the essential starting point, as is the experience of journeying through it – responding, as Richard Long described it, to the earth moving beneath your feet. But the work is also about memory and time as much as what is seen – the memory of what was once there, as well as the memory of previous work done in same place. The paintings become a way of examining my own transient presence as well as the changing nature of the landscape itself. By way of example, when walking along a mountain trail you can see the path travelled yesterday stretching behind you and the day to come running ahead of you. In this sense time and space become synonymous.

The pictures record not only those ephemeral moments of personal submersion but also chart a deeper history, tracing out those often barely discernible fragments and stories (whose signs are often lost or barely discernible) that make up a place, the invisible yet palpable layers which lie within and beneath the surface. The rushing mountain stream I worked beside for a month in Vermont for example, was called the Gihon (named after one of the four mythical rivers of Eden) and seemed to contain within its flow the quiet language of the past.

As with my earlier desert paintings they combine the mapping out in space, on paper and canvas, of a physical journey with a kind of cultural excavation that speaks of duration, time passing. This experience was especially acute in Vermont where I set out to create a visual diary by making one picture a day in one place over the course of a month as winter turned to spring. Despite these differing approaches and locations there is in all the work a sense of the present erasing the past, something physically manifest in the shadow lines left in the residue of coloured ink or the evidence of earlier drawings occasionally glimpsed through subsequent layers of paint. For the critic Nicholas Usherwood, writing about the work in 2009, it amounted to a continuous process of loss and recovery.

As for my work being described as 'abstract' or 'landscape' – I find them somewhat limiting terms – I'm more interested in working at the edge, or on the margins of both. There is always a fixed starting point in time and place, a relation to the exterior world of phenomena that allows for a dialogue with an interior space of recollection and feeling, but this is less to do with 'taking in' a landscape as the idea of 'landscape' itself and what this means in relation to other times and cultures. Early on I was fascinated by the desert paintings of aboriginal Australians, images that were read at the time by a western audience as abstract patterns but which in fact directly recounted their experience of walking over ancestral ground. They did not paint the horizon because they could not touch it.

My aim likewise is to be as receptive to the surface of the visual field I'm moving across as what lies unseen beneath it. The paintings grow out of particular encounters with places both distant and near, and the subsequent marks deployed on canvas and paper can be read as hieroglyphic texts – or even as maps of the 'geographical unconscious' – that set out to evoke both the trail of our presence and the passage of time. They place, as Odilon Redon once put it, 'the logic of the visible in the service of the invisible' –

'la logique du visible au service de l'invisible'.

Luke Elwes

e.

The end of the Essex way was marked on the High Lighthouse, which ceased operation in the nineteenth-century. Harwich had seen three pairs of lighthouses fall into disuse. The first were wooden and the last, on the seafront at Dovercourt, were made of cast iron. From the promenade near the latter, D____ searched to see Fort Roughs, the World War Two Maunsell Sea Fort, which in 1967 became the micronation of Sealand.

The Optimist

All he wanted was a little square.
3,000 feet of fertile air
And the whole of the cut – glass Fenland sky –
Just for a bit, until he died.
The moon sang on
Those full-bodied nights they shared and
Reeling him to hedgerows cut with swords
She said how he could change the world.
For if this land was a woman, she said,
You two could bear the sweetest fruits upon the earth,
and know the words
This land is yours, this land is ours

All rag and bone they lay, unswept;
A stinging salt dipped itch between
The land and sea; depressed by the tsunami sky that
Sucks you up, you shingle left – for they have
Pulled The Plug on life, compressed our bones with fishing nets.

But the world is ripping out of its seams, the trees are
coming back to us,
Ripping
pavements over town and showing girls
With couch-lock frowns
Their hunchbacked roots.

Like zombies rising from the grave they break their
concrete chains and say
This land is ours, this land is yours

All wage and war they cried, bereft, a
Herd within its grid between
Their land and death – but somehow less –
For they have signed Progression's lines,
Compressed our bones for ***cattle flesh****.*

Tired of living in a long dark corridor, he said
He longed to be outside, to feel the beating heart behind
The pillared gates, reclaim the sand
That give the city spires reach,
A fickle beach is this old town
When money sings it's pretty round.
For if this city was a woman, he said,
She would be mean and she'd be vain and we would
Sweat and long to say
This land is ours, this land is yours.

Poppy Kleiser

Digger

We have a new neighbour. Just over our back hedge, behind a few trees, there is a close-packed bunch of bungalows. Council houses, they used to be called. Social housing now.

An old, irritable lady used to live in the nearest one with her hyperactive, irritable dog. She moved out to a smaller place in a nearby village, taking her dog but leaving her small but well-tended, much-loved garden.

Though prickly as a blackthorn she'd bonded with my girl over plants; both obsessed with growing things, the pensioner had shared her age-won wisdom and her saved seeds, donated cuttings and identified weeds. Then one day after a few too many cups of strong tea and under the baleful influence of the *Daily Mail*, an argument had flared about, oh, immigration, crime, foreigners, something. One of those hair-trigger topics. Words were spoken, then a long stubborn silence.

They mended their differences awkwardly and slowly over time. The old lady wasn't one to bend. Stilted but sincere good wishes were exchanged on her departure.

Then the house lay fallow for a few months, before a single mum and her young brood arrived, bringing a noisy townie boyfriend and his Transit van. The kids screamed, he shouted, she screeched and the music thumped; an odd unthinking mix of Oasis, The Prodigy and Bon Jovi, a taste unified only by its beery antisociality and empty bombast. A spattering of emptied Stella cans rained over the hedge, while fires were lit on the once-weeded lawn and the bird table was kicked to rotting splinters and tossed in a corner.

Words were had, occasionally. By us, by other neighbours, by the police sometimes. Not much changed. And then everything did. They were gone after one final defiant bonfire, leaving a pile of sodden, scorched MDF that had once been a child's desk flung over our hedge with an empty bottle of cheap vodka. Impossible to tell whether that had been used as drink or accelerant. It would have worked either way.

Then vacancy for months; no-one lived in the bungalow while the year's wet winter came to drench the garden's debris again and again. And as it does, nature crept back to reclaim and repair. Soon enough the aconites were printing their sun-yellow asterisks like footnotes in the margins of the lawn and the grape hyacinths were poking up purple liquorice allsort heads. Though untended and straggling, the rosemary hedge flowered palest Wedgwood blue and the trellis-tied quince a startling scarlet.

The old lady never came back. She'd walked away, stubborn as a stone, head held rigid, and stated that she wouldn't return. No point, she asserted. Don't look back. She'd probably never listened to Bob Dylan, and wouldn't have liked it if she had. He would have liked her. She had everything she needed and she didn't look back, not once.

Her garden kept flowering on despite her permanent absence, showing off to nobody at all, framing the blank-eyed bungalow. Peering over the hedge, if you ignored the burnt patch in the middle of the lawn it looked like a pleasant place; a little patch of England where you could sit out on a cloudy summer day and sip PG Tips at your wrought-iron-effect B&Q garden table while Radio Four burbled away to itself.

And as Radio Four often does, let's digress. Let's add some background in here. Imagine it being read in the plummy, earnest Radio Four Documentary Voice, if you like.

We live, on most weekends and at other odd times, in a converted barn in Norfolk. The rest of the time we inhabit an East London live/work studio space. We're both in the sort of occupations usually classed as 'creative & media'.

Yes, I know how that sounds. Granite worktops and a labradoodle. Organic farmers' market on a Saturday, never anywhere to park the Range Rover. Kids called Thomas and Petunia, dove grey Farrow & Ball paint everywhere. Great mates with Polly Fucking Toynbee and Alan Fucking Yentob.

It's not that. The barn's a shed with slightly better insulation. Small, about the size of a council semi or a London terrace, but with fewer walls inside. There's a functional kitchen and a cheap wood stove; a bed up in the old hayloft and a gang of scrappy hedge sparrows living under the roof eaves at the front.

But it's in a couple of acres of its own meadow, ringed by

trees planted as saplings only a decade and a half ago and now grown into proper full-sized whitebeams, wild cherries and field maples.

There's a pond we dug painfully out of the flint-filled clay and a gravel-topped garden where we grow beans and peas up wigwams made out of our own hazel sticks, inexpertly coppiced and roughly held together with hairy string.

The garden's full of sea holly and marigolds, primroses and oregano, fennel and honesty; a random straggle of plants who've elbowed their way in and found claggy, rich soil topped with pea gravel to their liking.

And it's in Norfolk. But not North Norfolk, that Islington-on-Sea preserve of artisan chutney makers. This is South Norfolk. We don't have twee towns with matt olive-green shopfronts full of local watercolourists' dauby beachscapes, driftwood seagull sculptures and vanilla-scented candles. We have places called Mr Overalls and Farmbits Direct; shops that sell rat poison and paraffin, towropes and tarpaulins. The local newsagents stock copies of *Classic Tractor* magazine and though there's a long Norfolk tradition of making craft cider, nobody local drinks that muck. The off-licences specialise in one-pint cans of Stella. Maybe a bottle of Lambrini for the wife.

This is functional countryside. When professional eco-contrarian George Monbiot, writing on agriculture, used the phrase 'Norfolk's chemical desert', this was the bit he meant. Crops here are the ugly, profitable ones, planted intensively and sprayed persistently. Sugar beet, maize, lurid hazard-warning yellow rape, all on an unforgiving cycle where one is planted the moment another is harvested.

The soil doesn't get much chance to lie fallow here; it's a resource to be utilised industrially, efficiently. Get a subsidy for leaving the margins unplanted? Leave them then. Subsidy discontinued? Plough and spray right to the edge. It's all about profit. That's it. No room for stupid towny ideas like wildlife and sustainability. The environment? What's that? Can you eat it or drive it or spend it?

The odd bits you'll find unploughed are for sheltering game birds, bred to be shot in vast numbers by parties of the rich and well-connected, dressed in bright new tweed and attended by respectful keepers and beaters. Which century is it again? Never mind.

And between the vast hedge-grubbed fields are eyewateringly ammoniac chicken sheds supplying worryingly cheap poultry for supermarket ready meals and gigantic piggeries with a stench so powerful as to be almost physically tangible.

This is exactly the kind of countryside in which I spent much of my childhood. I hated it.

When I was just old enough for school my parents left their London roots and moved to Nottinghamshire, where my father had found work. I can't blame them; it was a good job, with a respected company. In search of an affordable house, they'd found a new estate in a rural village and bought a modern red-brick detached. Again, I can't blame them; it was a nice house, with a nice garden and nice neighbours. Mostly.

As Londoners do, they had a rather rose-tinted view of the countryside; it was, they thought, healthier and happier than the dirty, crowded city they'd left. Ironically, for several weeks every summer the nearby rose grower squirted rank-smelling fish manure over his crop, making the country infinitely more odoriferous than even Soho's grubbiest alleys.

Summer was manure smells and itchy thunderflies, winter was endless drizzle and nothing on telly.

And the locals were obsessed with being the locals. We spoke funny because we'd come up from London, so we'd never be locals. This was made very clear in the pubs and the shops and every time we talked to somebody born in the village. They were real local people, the salt of the earth, the keepers of some unspoken tradition to do with speaking in their local accent and knowing the other local people and who they were related to locally and who owned which patch of local ground. And we weren't and never would be. You're not from round here, we would be told, sometimes kindly, as though that was a sad medical deficit, a psychogeographical handicap.

Then sometimes the grubbier part of that attitude would show itself – where localism slides into xenophobia and pride becomes racism. Mutterings about 'gypsies' and 'pikeys' and 'niggers' and 'pakis' and 'gays' and 'them'. Heavy emphasis on the word 'them', meaning anyone but the locals, a formless threatening otherness born of ignorance, fear and distrust.

This wasn't the welcoming, rose-covered cottage, chocolate-box Enid Blyton countryside, this was proper unpleasantness; malice and stupidity mingled with inbreeding and resentment. The gossip was pointed, the prejudices permanent. This was why I hated the country.

What's more, I missed the lights and the people of London, the activity and the anonymity. I was, frankly, bored shitless.

As soon as possible I escaped the country and returned to London. And that, I thought, was that. No more manure for me.

Then somehow, thanks to that combination of practicality and love, attraction and compromise that makes up a relationship, I ended up in the country again for at least part of the time; in a small barn in the middle of a field in South Norfolk.

And one day, next to that barn, we had new neighbours.

A van and a gang of people, clumped around a tracksuited, straggle-blonde woman with a set jaw and a deep-eyed scowl. We said hello, as you do.

She eyed us warily, while her two-man entourage (middle-aged bloke, dark, thickset; older bloke, dark, thickset) scowled from behind their hefted leatherette sofa. She had dogs, she told us. But she was going to put a fence up so they wouldn't get out and cause a nuisance. So that was fine then. Good. Hope you like the new house. We knew the old lady who used to live here; she loved that garden. You'll enjoy sitting out there when the grass has had a chance to grow back. She nodded.

The following weekend, noises. Flashing lights. Mechanical revvings and roarings. Creaks and thumps. A small excavator had arrived, driven by the middle-aged thickset bloke; her brother. He was bluff but friendlier this time. He was local, he said. All the family were. The older bloke was their father, he lived up the village too. His sister had lived in Norwich, but her only son had died suddenly so she'd returned to the village to put her life back together. Shame, we said. Tell her we're very sorry. As you do.

He was clearing the boundary line so they could put that fence up, he said. For the dogs. Leave as much of the greenery as you can, I asked. He would, he said. He loved trees himself, he said. Fine. He wouldn't make much mess; this was what he did for a living. We'll leave you to it then. Hope it goes well.

At lunchtime more noises; the throaty diesel of a flat-bed lorry arriving to pick up the digger's debris.

Then, swiftly and surgically, the excavator cleared the entire garden and dumped it into the truck. The quince on its trellis, the rosemary hedge and the aconites; tulips just budding and crocus bulbs plumping up for next year, daffodils and fruit bushes. Even the lawn. All of it gone, scraped and scoured down to bare turd-brown earth, the long-nurtured plants now landfill, shovelled expertly on to the lorry and carted away in a rumble of exhaust.

When she first saw the ruins of her neighbour's garden,

my girl stopped dead and whimpered wordlessly, tears brimming. The family were still there, looking on. Sister stood arms folded, defiant. My garden, she said, knowing exactly what the sobs had meant, I can do what I like with it.

Brother, sensing a storm, busied himself loading his excavator on to a trailer.

Father came forward, eyes narrowed, belligerent, defensive. We know all about you, he said. You're from London. You live in that old barn. We've been in this village all our lives.

We knew all about the last people who had this house too, he accused. Pikeys they were. Bad as gypsies, them people. Them diddies, they don't deserve a house.

You don't have any right to tell us what to do, he raged, though we hadn't said a word. We've been in this village all our lives.

Anyway, you're not from round here. You don't understand the country.

He turned and stumped off after that last word, inarguable and final. You're not from round here. You don't understand the country.

Chris Maillard

The Boots in the Dunes

(Burnham Overy Staithe)

White Converse have their toehold in the dunes
a hallowed spot where windscour whips their heels
silk-sand laps at tongues and laceholes
bootmouths open to the sky
as though some Foreign Legionnaire
has stumbled to these Norfolk drifts
has thrown his kepi up into the air
let go his rifle and his pack
to plunge through sweeps of sand and marram grass
down to the mirage of the sea
to feel salt eddies cool his desert heat
to lave and soothe his blistered hands and feet
and leave his boots to Norfolk and the dunes.

Peter Kennedy

f.

A bull had chased two ramblers across the field into a ditch in the grazing marsh. We had approached the brackish water seeking hydrophilus piceus, the great silver water beetle that was occasionally spied near Shotley. The looming cranes in the distance reminded D____ of the huge wealth of Trinity College, Cambridge, which owned much of the land on which Felixtowe's container port was built. There was a skylark overhead.

The Deep South

For someone born in the mid-west of Essex in the 1950s, Southend was the deep south – a combination of seaside-iness and mystery. It was the East End on sea, the urban daring of salty life, associated with big pubs, the darkest blues, the longest pier. There were still Teddy Boys in Southend, with big Ford Consuls. Kiss-me-quick is a cliché, but one that evokes the romance and sudden wildness of the sea and a sharp dedication to pleasure. That sense of a potent atmosphere, of dangerous, seductive intensity has remained, but with more subtle, swampy shades thrown in.

In the 1970s, as a singer and songwriter in folk clubs, I was tuned into an English music hall vibe that chimed with what was happening in the rock music scene you could read about in the *New Musical Express* and *Melody Maker*. There was an English flavour in local bands like the Kursal Flyers that was not lost on me. I performed my songs in Southend Folk Club, where rock songwriter legend Mickey Jupp (whose band was even called Legend) sometimes turned up to play. By then I was also influenced by Canvey Island's own Dr Feelgood – had seen them live several times. My very English, music hall influenced songs were short and to the point like theirs. The quickness and the liveliness was my small corner of making Essex resonate.

The great traditional English folksinger Nic Jones was another favourite at the time. On the surface, the brash, electric Feelgoods and the careful, acoustic Jones were opposites. But they both had an English quality, an Essex intensity even. Nic was from Chelmsford. I remember doing a seasidey song, 'Knickerbocker Glory', at a club in south Essex when Nic was top of the bill. He told me he liked it. If I was doing something different, it felt like Essex's openness would not reject it.

In the 1980s I joined The Metric Foot Band, a Maldon-based folk-rock English barndance band. They're still going. We played all over Essex – gigs on Canvey and outdoors at the Leigh-on-Sea Folk Festival. At Canvey I got chatting to some kids by the side of the stage and one told me his Uncle John was Sparko, the original Feelgoods bassist. Around this time too, I had a rare sighting of their songwriter and guitarist Wilco Johnson.

Driving back home through Westcliff one day I saw Wilco pushing a pram. He was dressed in exactly the same clothes he wore on stage. This seemed not only deeply impressive, but somehow reassuring. He was so much himself, which, I felt, gave me license somehow to be as much myself as I wanted. Wilco still seems to inspire such epiphanies.

In the following decade I wrote a story about a disillusioned rock musician while taking an MA in Creative Writing. The protagonist was a band's bass player who hated his over-playing lead guitarist. Like me, he sees Wilco going about his daily life, completely, utterly himself. The character is reassured and realises he can carry on. Something powerful and promising was there, still.

John Banyard, who founded the Essex religious sect The Peculiar People, was from Rochford and had been a drunken satirical songwriter, who woke in a ditch, naked and penniless, before taking up his primitive, evangelical new religion in the mid nineteenth century. 'Peculiar' is a Biblical reference and means 'chosen'. I read a book about them by Mark Sorrell (*The Peculiar People*, 1980). Writing my songs, I sought out the locally intense, those with the quickness of life and the possibility of change. Cunning Murrell of Hadleigh was another of those deep south magicians. He was a real witch character, written into a novel by Arthur Morrison (*Cunning Murrell*, 1900).

Just a few years back, making a radio programme called 'Dr Adrian May's Artistic Navigation Device of Essex', I interviewed the poet Martin Newell, the writer Ronald Blythe, plus my friend and bandmate, the traditional folksinger Sue Cubbin, as well as Wilco Johnson. All, in their very different ways, reflected on a kind of immersive relationship with their Essex places, which was a source of creative energy, like the one I had sought and been nourished by. Wilco and I posed as the radio producer took a mobile phone photo of us – two mad-eyed, rough Essex intellectuals stood together.

Living in north Essex and teaching creative writing at university, I still get to talk about these things. I still try to get that kind of Essex defiance and energy into my songs and poems. The University has a place in Southend, so my links and inspiration from the deep south have not been neglected. In fact, I have a plan to make them stronger:

To anyone who will listen, I tell them we need a university boat. Then we can get in touch with our geography, our coast, our deep south links. I imagine readings and gigs on the boat, as we go north to south, Colchester to Southend, waving to Clacton and Maldon: psychogeography lessons, parties and big skies. They would have to re-open Colchester's port at Hythe, though. It's where I live and I'd need to be able to dock at the end of the pier. Obviously. Easy.

In the plan, I'm the captain, describing the shape of Essex daily, somehow in constant touch with that quick, fluid sharpness of creativity and able to communicate that to everyone on board, from the high north to the deep south.

Adrian May

From Island to Bay

(for Mehalah)

You were a girl of seven or so
bred on east coast saltings
your home, *The Victor*, nestled in sea mud
your purview Mersea's sundry folk
when I saw you last on moving stairs at Baker Street
before your *Fairsea* passage to the far antipodes.

Removed, you said, from hemisphere to hemisphere
– estuary's black water to the shark blue of the Bay;
transplanted, you said, from the Island's heavy clay
to François Peron's red peninsula.

But you being Baring-Gould's girl
kept the Strood, the Ray, and the *Rose* in view
– would remove them to Denham
where you potted cross-legged girls
or painted sea-grass swirling,
these to be marvelled at by travellers in your quayside studio.

Now you bring full cups to the *Cloud's* two tables
where Denham's denizens come to read in the Bay's breeze
or gather for conversation as convivial as *Fountain, Victory,* and *Lion*,
haunts of the Mussetts, Wyatts and de Witts
who with raised glasses drank to the men as the smacks came in.

But alack!
You found the Bay's hot winds, red earth's dust, and
unpeopled places
belied the Island's creeks, its channels and North Sea chills,
its characters, contours and yesterdays,
and could not match pleasant Mersea memory
with the all-too-plain present of Shark Bay.

Antony Johae

S. Baring-Gould is the author of the novel Mehalah: A Story of the Salt Marshes *(1880).*
Denham is located in Shark Bay, Western Australia.

g.

The ship's company was formed in the 1980s to carry chemicals between the UK and Poland. Today its fleet sails between Russia (Sint-Petersburg), Poland (Szczecin, Gdansk, Gdynia), the UK (Flixborough, Howdendyke, Boston, Seaham, London, Goole), Ireland (Drogheda, Belfast), Belgium (Antwerp, Ghent) and the Netherlands (Flushing, Rotterdam). The ships also call at other European ports on a 'sufficient inducement' basis. In this case, D____ adduced that 'sufficient inducement' had been proffered.

Three Sorts of Sunshine

At Frinton seafront, I searched for a place to begin. The grass sucked at my feet and the sky was grey. Seagulls sipped from a puddle. The view was marked with patches of scrub, vacant wooden benches and a cylindrical seating hut. At the pinnacle of the hut's roof, four clock faces seemed to say 'time is important here'. It was cold. Human life appeared absent, represented only with its properties, its cars, its financial trappings.

I passed the squabbling seagulls in search of sand. Three flights of salt-battered steps dissected three rows of correctly proportioned beach huts. A crushed beer can, then a bunch of them, broke the ranks. At the bottom, my feet met the concrete of a promenade. Ethereal dog walkers seemed to step out from the driftwood along the shore.

I leaned against the sea wall. Along the skyline stood a white offshore wind farm, its metronome blades swinging to nature's rhythm. The sea was out, the sun pushed through, and the polished sand gleamed. I turned toward the beach huts. Stained in colours of olive-green, earth-brown and royal-blue, summer was entombed behind their boarded windows and rusting padlocks. It seemed a dismal camp of concentrated absence. Further on, the huts had advanced onto the shore, towering over me on metal legs of ten feet or more. I stood in line with them, close to legs covered in black seaweed.

Inland, the scene was moulded for golf. On a sculpted grass landscape, Lowry figures swung their clubs by an elevated concrete promenade. To my right a cycle path, a ditch and the golf course; to my left, a sea-wall and the encroaching tide. Pushing into a breeze, I reached a World War Two pillbox camouflaged by age. It was overlooked by a pylon, and its watchtower dominance seemed to be where the Haven and Holland-on-Sea began. I stretched to peer over the wall. The sea had swallowed the beach while rocks were busy throwing it back. The way ahead was a frontline where the authority of Frinton appeared to end.

*

Where subdued Holland-on-Sea finally drops off to sleep, I leaned against a cold metal rail and smiled at the offshore turbines. The steep cliff face to the promenade was covered in prickly plants and, along the foreshore, the sea was at low tide. Gulls squabbled over scraps of fast food. Between their cries I heard human yells. On seats next to a metal-shuttered ice cream kiosk, two young men and a woman puffed on cigarettes and chomped on chips. I had arrived at Clacton.

I walked down a sloping pathway and continued along the promenade in the direction of the pier. Workmen up ladders repaired buildings that had suffered the weather's wrath. A couple of hospital staff took a break from work, their language rich with migrated phrases and vocabulary.

Mobility vehicles cruised dogmatically past. As I reached the pier, the song of nature sank below songs from the local radio station, Dream 100, its speakers playing tracks from the Eighties. I sat on a concrete wall to listen. From behind came competing noise: the Pavilion Bowl punched out a rave.

On the smooth and bare sand, figures with metal-detectors hunted for treasure. A large cafeteria refreshed a huddle of seaside-postcard tubby women. Hibernating businesses seemed close to waking. Carved into the cliff face, an alcove provided wooden benches. A mural covered its sheltering wall – graffiti art told the history of Clacton and of an acceptance of modernity. I unscrambled the references: a goddess flew the banner Mighty Clactonia above mammoth bones, smugglers, Edwardian and Victorian figures, soldiers, a goofy Butlin-coated lady and mods on scooters.

Along the narrowing embankment I stopped at a set of pristine beach huts, perfect clones in structure but each with its own character. Cottage garden hues of rosy pink, lilac and daffodil yellow, illuminated the rocky setting. At street level, the West Greensward featured large timber seating huts, a playground, a small pool for model yachts and a set of ornamental gardens with names such as Sunken Rose, Sensory, Mediterranean and Memorial. In the gardens, hedges and trees muffled the sounds of traffic and the sight of bucket-and-spade laden tourists. It was a secret garden, its isolating calm only snatched away by another discovering the secret. Nature had provided a succession of mirages, places of contemplation. Respect was symbolised by bench plaques of dead relatives, dedications to military associations and poppy wreaths. At the centre of the Memorial Garden was an angel of peace, a memorial to those who died in the First and Second World Wars. Blood-red paper poppies encased a padlock: respect keeping its handshake intact.

I crossed the wide curving concrete bridge that strides the road leading to the pier. A static fairground snoozed under a chained tarpaulin, its animation drained until summer plugged it back in, its attractions cloaked in flapping canvas. I had the sensation of being watched. I glanced upwards. At the top of a shrouded mound, a white-bearded hillbilly looked down. His manufactured presence was jumping-for-joy, holding a shovel below the attraction name: Gold Diggers!

*

I arrived at Martello Bay, Jaywick, on a bracingly cold afternoon. This historic monument was once a fort dating back to the Napoleonic era. Its forty-foot dominance stubby and round, its thick masonry skin peeling. There were windows built for cannon fire, boarded up.

On the beach, the re-seeded sand lay in soft mounds. Sunk into its dunes was a resting tractor, its bucket used to control the beach if it misbehaved. As distance left the tower behind the coast became feral. Sand formed into a hilly terrain. On top of the mounds tufts of green grass sprouted like hairy moles on old ladies' chins. I followed the promenade until the hamlet of Jaywick Sands came into view, to where Jaywick seafront officially begins, or ends, in thick bramble and a sign saying 'Golf Club Property. Keep Out'.

From here, the concrete promenade turns into an alley that runs between Jaywick beach and converted beach huts. These dwellings are hybrid – a mix of red-brick garden walls and pixieland roofs. On the sand was a large cream and blue wooden shack, announcing itself as a beach bar, its serving hatches sealed with ice-cream adverts. Next to it was a sand-submerged speed boat.

In the distance, an amusement arcade had the word 'Wonderland' across its front. There were beach huts with the life blown out of them. One carcass was the shape of a long pentagon. In its youth it probably served as a summer holiday retreat which at some stage had become permanent. Now there were glassless windows and a hole that was once a door. Inside was a quaint fireplace and an arch that led to a mildew-decorated room. With the roof missing, it was a grave robbed by nature.

Further along the beach were two large boulders with plaques from the Environment Agency, commemorating the defence work in 1990 by the local flood committee. A cream Art Deco building with the title 'Amusements' was the gateway to Brooklands. The six-foot high concrete defence that ran along Brooklands' seaward side was known locally as Adrian's Wall, named after the chairman of freeholders association who paid for it after the floods of 1953.

The tarmacked road led to a succession of makeshift streets, each named after cars: Hillman, Rover, Bentley, Austin and Sunbeam: a reminder that the chalets here were built and colonised by workers from the Ford plant in Dagenham. But as the idea of the country retreat lost currency, the bustling holiday village became, superficially, a wreck. Here, roads led to eroded gullies, pockmarked and awash with water. Residents' cars were parked up sloping verges and caravans paddled.

Near the Mermaid Inn, now gagged with chipboard, breeze blocks and splitting plywood, I paid my respects to happy times. People had embraced their homes here. There was mock Tudor and a white, Irish-themed bungalow complete with green clover and leprechauns. Beach huts that had transformed into cosy bungalows. Perished wood was replaced with double glazing, mouldy exteriors traded for painted pebbledash, soggy mattresses and armchairs in front gardens exchanged for raised beds, borders and boats. There were many boats in Jaywick, on the beach and in peoples' gardens. I thought of the 1953 floods that took the lives of thirty-five people. Who can tell if these boats might be needed again?

I stopped to listen to the sea. Behind me was a newly built housing estate on the site where Butlin's Holiday

Camp once stood, and where my parents met, my mum selling souvenirs and my dad frying doughnuts. As a small child, I would enviously peer at the giant man and the miniature train ride. Excited yelps and happy tunes played in my head, an experience witnessed again from afar. And on the beach again, sea defences came in the form of a wall of large rocks, like Frinton's giant beach huts, their hardness softened by seaweed.

Jennifer Walford

The Kindness of Strangers

I graduated from the University of Essex in 1997, just after 'New' Labour won the election, and I returned to London. That next four years saw such decadence, friends running up enormous sums of money on their credit cards and night after night downing cocktails. There were many times when I felt uncomfortable on those graduate social sessions, uneasy with the excess, unsettled by the endless talk of acquisition and salaries. On one night my associates were talking about all us being characters from *The Great Gatsby*, christening us Jay, Jordan, Daisy and Myrtle, I couldn't help contemplating the irony of this; after all, wasn't all the fun of the roaring Twenties ended by the desolation of the Great Depression?

The *Gatsby* comment really got under my skin: memories of German Expressionist paintings played on my mind, thoughts of Steinbeck's *The Grapes of Wrath* and Dorothea Lange's 'Migrant Mother' haunted me. I remembered my cause and effect sessions in GCSE history and that the reason why the Great Depression hit both the rich and poor of America and Germany was that everyone was in dept to everybody else – I was being overly simplistic, sure, but wasn't that the case now? Hadn't anyone learned anything?

Then the crash came.

This time some lessons had supposedly been learned from history. Banks were bailed this time, the rich were saved and all the middle had to do tighten their belts and sit tight. Austerity chic became *de rigueur*, 'make do and mend' and 'grow your own' were fashionable phrases and 'second hand' morphed into 'vintage'. So who was really suffering? You don't have to be an historical expert to know that the real victims of any economic downturn are the poor. In fact, a June 2014 report by Oxfam, Trussell Trust and Church Action on Poverty, highlighted the scale of the problem, finding that more than half a million children in the UK were living in families that were unable to provide a minimally acceptable diet.

The poor haven't had good press of late. Over recent years I've become depressed by so-called poverty porn TV shows such as *The Jeremy Kyle Show*, *Benefits Street* and *On Benefits & Proud* and saddened by characters such as *Little Britain's* Vicky Pollard and *Shameless'* Frank Gallagher. I see these TV 'favourites' as pernicious, insidious ways to demonise those who have nothing. I think the propaganda has worked; in my comfortable world of work as a writer and editor, derogatory words about 'council house scum' and terms such as 'chav', 'pikey' and 'charva' have been casually bandied about in every office I've been in over the past ten years. There are times when I've felt that it's a crime to be poor – or at least that there's a perception that if you are poor you probably deserve it.

I have a vested interest in this. I grew up on a council

estate in London's Hackney in the Eighties and early Nineties. That sentence automatically reveals my economic background. But how about if I were to have grown up in Norwich? What does that reveal? My experience of Norwich and the surrounding areas has always been pleasant. My sister went to the University of East Anglia and enjoyed her three years in the city. My parents lived for a while in a beautiful flint-covered cottage in North Norfolk. As far as I've been concerned, that part of the world was safe, privileged and affluent. So I was surprised to read a February 2013 report by Campaign to End Child Poverty that Norwich is in the top five per cent of authorities in the UK for child poverty. The same report named the city as having the highest percentage of children in poverty in the East of England, with the wards of Mile Cross, Wensum, Mancroft, Bowthorpe, University and Lakenham as having more than one in three children living in poverty. I never grew up in poverty, I did not go hungry, but children in Norwich are.

If the popular media is to be believed, there's no such thing as poor people, simply scroungers who sponge of the state and get fat on junk food. So much so that research entitled *The Lies We Tell Ourselves: Ending Comfortable Myths About Poverty*, published by the Baptist Union of Great Britain, the Church of Scotland, Methodist and United Reformed Churches, found that more than eighty per cent of the UK population believe that large numbers falsely claim benefit. Interestingly, the paper also reports that in-work poverty is now more common than out of work poverty.

In the twelve months ended 28 February 2014, Norwich food bank provided 9,614 local people (including 3,149 children) with three days' worth of food. Compare this to 6,042 people who asked for help during the twelve months to 28 February 2013 and you'll see an increase of around fifty-nine per cent, year-on-year. I asked Norwich food bank project manager Grant Habershon what circumstances drive people to come to the food bank: "There are so many," he says. "There are often delays in the benefits process, so people are left with periods when they simply have no money coming in and can't buy even the most basic of foods. A sudden crisis such as bereavement, redundancy or illness, can leave them unable to feed themselves or their families. If you have no safety net, no friends or family to support you, where can you go? Such situations can quickly deteriorate, leading to relationship breakdown, house repossession or worse."

He continues: "We also meet a lot of families who work but are simply on low incomes. A lot of our parents regularly miss meals so that their children can do sport or hobbies that will keep them off the streets. Others tell us about how they have to inform their children that they cannot afford a school trip or even to have a friend round for tea. We also see a massive increase in referrals every August when children are on school holidays and are therefore no longer eligible for free school meals."

You can't just turn up at Norwich food bank. Normally you are referred by a professional. If someone arrives unreferred, food bank staff put them in touch with relevant local agencies who can assess their need and "signpost them to the right services". Personally, I'm uncomfortable with the notion of people having to prove that they're hungry and desperate, but according to Habershon the referral system is a good thing. "Because people can't simply walk in off the street the local community know that the need is genuine. Everybody has been remarkably generous, from local people to supermarkets. I've been astonished by the support everyone has shown us and continues to do so. I'm so proud of the people in this city," he says.

"We work closely with local care organisations whose professional care-workers identify people in crisis, give them a food voucher and refer them to one of our distribution centres. Here they are given a warm welcome, a hot drink and a nutritionally balanced emergency food box to cover an individual or family's basic needs for seventy-two hours. If they wish, our visitors can also benefit from a listening ear and help in finding other professionals who can assist them with the underlying problems that is causing their crisis," Habershon explains.

"Sometimes a vulnerable person or family can deal with so many different organisations that those who work for them don't realise that a delay at one stage in the process can have really damaging effects along the line. For example, there is an enormous needs for nappies, especially for newborns, but if a birth isn't registered then a parent can't be referred. If we can talk to the different agencies then we can hopefully get some more joined-up thinking. That's why our links with the community and care agencies are so important."

My conversation with Habershon made me look closer to home to find out what's happening in the nearest big town to where I live, Colchester. I spoke to Linda Hurr, Colchester food bank manager. In 2013, the bank fed 2,900 people, 900 of whom were children. Based on the first six months of 2014, the organisation expects to feed approximately 5,870 people over the year, 2,612 of whom will be children.

"Many more families, and therefore children, are falling below the poverty line in 2014," says Hurr. "Demand quadrupled last year and it's still on the increase. We now distribute more than five tonnes of food (approximately eighty parcels a week) every month. During our first five years of operation we distributed fifty-three tonnes of food, but this year we are likely to do this amount in just ten months."

Colchester food bank currently has more than fifty volunteers who help with collections, manning events, sorting out food donations and making up emergency parcels. The organisation is mostly funded by the community, both in terms of food and finances.

As with the Norwich food bank, people are referred by external care agencies. Just like Norwich, Hurr cites the largest group needing the Bank's services as those whose benefit has been delayed, cut or sanctioned and who are left with no income for several weeks. Recently, however, Hurr has also seen a significant increase in families referred due to low income or zero hour contracts: "An unexpected bill in these circumstances can be catastrophic. These issues can lead to people becoming trapped in debt and getting ill due to poor nutrition. The stress and anxiety of such a situation can lead to depression and other mental health problems. Some of our visitors have developed addictions and become involved with criminal activities to fund their addictions. Many clients are not aware of the support that is available and need help accessing it. When people come to us they often feel isolated, vulnerable, excluded, worthless, hopeless and despairing. Irritability and even anger can result, all exacerbated by hunger."

Like Habershon, Hurr is also keen to get agencies working more closely with one another. "By working together we can avoid duplication and resources can be used more effectively to provide our clients with a more holistic form of support," she says.

"It's a sad fact that it looks as though food banks are here to stay for the foreseeable future. We may even see a further increase in demand when the next ranch of welfare changes come into force," she explains. "We are therefore making plans for the sustainability of Colchester food bank for the next five years and looking at alternative income streams such as opening a charity shop and increasing fundraising support. I am working on a 'Better Together' project whereby organisations work together rather than in competition. We aim to be the default provider of emergency food in Colchester and supply homeless agencies such as Beacon House, the April Centre, Night Shelter, Soup Run and Women's Refuge, with bespoke food parcels to allow them to concentrate on their own missions. I have recently obtained funding to run free courses for clients and these will include such things as confidence building and workplace skills. I have also recently set up an Essex Forum of food banks where can get together to network, discuss issues and generally support each other across the county."

I'm impressed and thankful for the fact that local people and businesses contribute time, money and stock to help others. But I can't help feeling troubled that local authority and official government agencies are passing people on to charities to sort out the situation rather than tackle it itself. It scares me that it is really only the kindness of strangers that is stopping people starving.

I feel like we're going backwards. The State doesn't appear to have a viable network of its own, nor does it seem to keen to put pressure on employers to give people a wage with which to feed themselves and their familes – it is simply outsourcing the problem.

This sense of going back in time rings particularly true for to me as I speak to Hurr. She tells me that the ethos of Colchester food bank is "to be God's Love in action", and that it was set up in October 2009 by Reverend Andrew Fordyce. It reminds me of the Charles Dickens' books I read when I was young, in which the only relief for those in need was from the Church or a kindly benefactor. Although I'm an atheist, I am incredibly mindful (and grateful) of the enormous part religious organisations have played in early health, welfare and education reform – it's their work, plus the contributions of well-meaning philanthropists, that paved the way for social housing and the establishment of the welfare state. Unfortunately it seems that, in the second decade of the twenty-first century, these very organisations are picking up the slack as wider society washes its hands of those in need.

Ella Johnston

Covehithe to Southwold

There on the cliff top lie the broken ribs of the church at Covehithe. Where once people prayed the wind whistles through empty pews. Here is a skeleton coast littered with the pale bones of the trees that once stood tall and now lie anchored in the soft sands. A floral spray of roots rest upon the high tide line: a wooden posy to the folk of Easton Broad – long departed Suffolk souls whose homes framed these sea-breeze fields. Halt a moment. Listen as you walk these empty beaches and you will hear their voices still – in the soft susurrus of the marsh grasses, in the swirling streams of sand that play at your feet as you walk beside the open underbelly of the cliff face. The sea will take all in time, they sigh.

James Canton

Water Birth

Made in the north,
I learned a hundred
words for rain, spooned
from my grandmother's lips.

She fed me pelt,
fur flattened by the deluge;
mizzle that settled
like mist on my tongue.

And then this place
where there's no need
for rain
because it's everywhere:

this estuary
gaping its teeth
to the sky,
spitting out herons
and egrets,
gargling swans like gutturals.

Strange how I belong here
– as if those northern factories

stitched flat skies
and seeping pools
through the textures of my skin.

Rosie Sandler

h.

It rained and we found shelter near the lime kiln. D____ commented that she had seen many entries in the *Victoria History of the Counties of England* in which similar kilns had been uncovered, revealing concealed treasures including Roman coins, Romano-British dark-ware Castor (Durobrivian) pottery and a vase decorated with scrolls and a female mask. It also made reference to bones, although it did not say whether they were human.

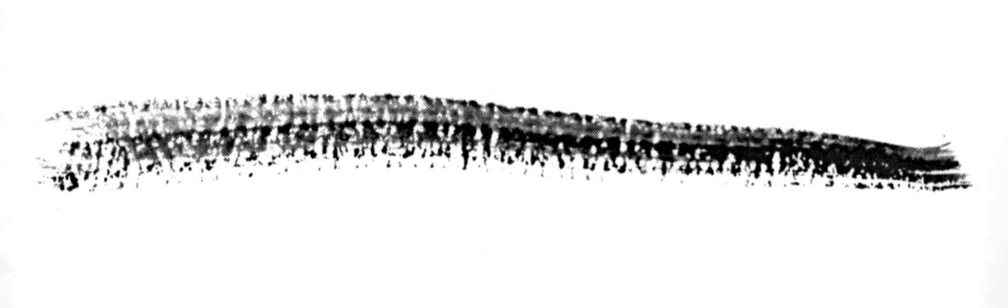

Living Landscape

An anonymous quote states that 'Essex is not flat and uninteresting; it is gently undulating and uninteresting'. I beg to differ.

I was born in West Horndon, near Upminster, but by the age of four was living in the village of Wormingford, on the Essex side of the Stour Valley, half way between Sudbury and Colchester. For me and my younger brother Kevin, this was a huge adventure. Our new home, Ingate House, was a derelict, sixteenth-century thatched cottage with a garden full of tangled vegetation tall enough to conceal us both from sight. At the centre of this jungle was a tall walnut tree in which Brian, our Dad, would later construct a tree-top platform for us to hold our secret club meetings.

But for now Ingate House was little more than a shell. The thatch was riddled with holes filled with nesting sparrows, the plaster hung from the wattle and daub in crumbling, dusty sheets and the window panes contained little more than fresh air. This lack of glass had allowed an industrious colony of bumblebees to set up home under one of the living room cupboards, and a pair of swallows had taken advantage of the main interior support beam to build a nest and raise a brood. Our first summer was characterised by the drone of flying insects and the rattling flight of birds passing through the empty window panes.

As time passed, however, the adventure began to wear

thin, and not just for my 25 year-old Mum, Gill, who was terrified of spiders (a fear she would later conquer after realising the spiders were not afraid of her). The only water in the house came from a cold-water standpipe in the hall and there was no gas or electricity so heating was limited to a small log fire. As winter arrived, trips to the garden shed to use the chemical toilet were often dark and dismal affairs. Thankfully, the living room was now secured against the elements after the departure of the birds and the bees, but I am constantly reminded that on visiting school friends in those first years, I would always ask my mum why we couldn't live in a 'normal' house.

Mum and Dad worked tirelessly on the cottage over the next few years. Electricity was installed, a real bathroom, a range for cooking and heating, and then, on a calm summer's day, a master thatcher arrived to repair the roof, a task which covered the whole village in straw for several weeks.

By the age of eight or nine, I began to realise just how lucky I was. I still wasn't keen on Dad's habit of surreptitiously installing snap traps around my bedroom, resulting in my sudden awakening at some ungodly hour as another unfortunate house mouse met its grisly end. But by now Kevin and I were part of a little group of children that spent their time exploring and mapping the hedges, fields and woods along the banks of the River Stour. And, my goodness, how we loved it.

This part of East Anglia has been immortalised by many

artists and writers. John Constable completed many of his most famous paintings in the Dedham Vale, and several of his relatives are buried in the Wormingford churchyard. But on the edge of the village, tucked away along a farm track, was a magical place for us all; Bottengoms. This was the home of Ronald Blythe, the author best known for *Akenfield*, his account of the inhabitants of a rural village in Suffolk in the 1960s, during a time of great agricultural and social change in the countryside. He would let us camp in his garden, occasionally bringing out trays of soft drinks, and we would play and explore the flower filled garden and little valley in which the cottage nestled.

Bottengoms itself was a treasure trove of paintings by Ronald's great friend, John Nash, who had bequeathed the cottage to Ronald on his death. At the time I had no concept of just what an important collection of paintings this was as they were simply everywhere. Many were on display but an even larger number leant against walls or were squirreled away around the house. It was a place that filled me with wonder and inspiration; a house that had taken root in the landscape and was part of the natural world rather than an intrusion upon it.

At first glance, my part of the Stour Valley appears to have changed very little since these childhood memories. When I drive to Wormingford from my new home in Holbrook, I usually follow the winding road that snakes along the Suffolk side of the valley through the beautiful villages of Stoke, Nayland and Wissington. This is a true country lane with passing places, twists and turns, bankside spoil heaps from burrowing badgers and views that remind me why people come here on holiday from all over the UK. And it is because of this love of the Stour valley and its hidden wonders that I suffer a particularly odd and personal recurring dream during times of personal stress. In it I stand horrified at the top of Wormingford hill looking down on a partially constructed six-lane motorway that has obliterated the landscape I knew as a child. I can't explain the flood of relief I experience upon waking.

And so, the seasons continue to march through the landscape with a palette of greens, browns, yellows, blues and purples. In the Seventies and Eighties, wide, steel-grey skies presaged winter snows that softened the land, filling the deeply entrenched lanes with six-foot drifts. The village would be cut off from the outside world for days until the snow receded enough for an army of local volunteers from the village to fight their way through to the Colchester Road behind a tractor fitted with a snow blade. Whilst we don't tend to experience deep drifts any more, winter snows still provide a blank canvas for the tracks of fox, brown hare and deer. Only the dry, nodding, flower-heads of tussocky cock's-foot grass peer out from the white blanket until the melt exposes a rash of bottle green rye-grass in the pastures once more.

The bluebell woods of Arger Fen burst into life in spring as dormice awaken from their winter slumbers. A private wood I knew well as a child, it is now under the stewardship of the Suffolk Wildlife Trust, along with much of the surrounding countryside, as it strives to preserve this 'Living Landscape'. Spring is a time of renewal in the valley. Once the snowdrops recede the mornings are filled with the sounds of the dawn chorus as males set up breeding territories and the first nests are built. There are still enough copses, hedgerows and pastures left to support sparrows, finches, yellowhammers and other farmland birds, but their numbers are considerably lower than they were when *Akenfield* was written.

Summer is a time of growth, as the river fills with the tall stems of Norfolk reed, branched bur-reed and the familiar cigar-shaped flower heads of reedmace – now often called bullrush. There are jewels to be found among the nettles here. Banded-demoiselles flutter up in clouds; the males a beautiful metallic blue with a dark 'thumbprint' mark on their otherwise clear wings. The broad-bodied powder-blue scarce chaser dragonfly, a new arrival on our river, emerges in large numbers to perch on the drooping flower-heads of pendulous sedge, looking for the next meal or the arrival of the orange and black females.

Calm autumn days are heralded by a change from green hedgerows to orange and gold as oak leaves carpet the hill behind Wormingford church. Birds and animals make haste to store as much of the autumn bounty away before the cold weather really takes hold. Wood mice pile up huge quantities of acorns in tree hollows or burrows while jays and squirrels just bury these precious seeds. Autumn also brings sudden storms and cloudbursts that sweep eastwards along the valley on stiffening winds. If out walking, Dad and I quicken our pace when we see them on the horizon, but the weather can turn quickly and if a storm takes the wrong track we return to Ingate House looking like a couple of drowned rats with soggy dogs in tow.

The landscape of 'Constable Country' can be deceptive. The pretty cloak disguises subtle changes from visiting eyes. The changes in farming practices and culture that Ronald Blythe documented in the Sixties have continued apace, as dairy pastures have been ploughed up for the production of potatoes, onions, oilseed rape and arable crops. The elms that so characterised the hedgerows of fifty years ago are gone and the late summer skies are no longer filled with the orange glow from blazing fields at the end of the harvest. I was part of the last generation of country children to witness the spectacular, but potentially ruinous, practice of stubble burning. We cycled along the valley 'fire chasing' the plumes of smoke while hoping for the excitement of a blaze that had hopped the rough ploughed fire-break along the field margins. I suppose at some stage it was decided that 'enough was enough' and our summer sport was brought to an abrupt halt.

Farming practices and pressures of human activity have certainly had an impact on the wildlife of the valley. The Stour was teeming with water voles when we had our makeshift raft moored up close to Wormingford bridge in the mid-Seventies, but the chances of seeing one there now are very slim, as they have been wiped out by farmed North American mink turned feral. Conversely, we would never have had the chance to disturb an otter whilst splashing around in the river back then as this iconic riverine predator had collapsed to near extinction due to pollutants from agricultural chemicals and road runoff. Thankfully, PCBs, DDT and leaded petrol were banned, allowing otters, the perfect barometer of the quality of our rivers, to breed successfully again.

Working on rivers is now my day job so I am delighted when I can take my work home and spend some time in the Stour valley. I have surveyed most of the valley, looking for solutions to restore the natural balance for the wildlife with which we shared the valley before the intensification of land-use caused such perilous declines. Unfortunately we will never witness the numbers of birds and animals we had in my Grandad's or even my Dad's youth as we simply do not have the quality or quantity of habitat, but we can still make a difference. Working on restoring water voles to our rivers has been a rewarding task. They are now reappearing along many stretches of the River Stour so I hope it won't be long before we hear the plop of tiny voles in Wormingford once more. We are also attempting to bypass the weirs and barriers that have carved the river up into a series of linear lakes, preventing the upstream migration of coarse fish and eels.

I know now that wherever I travel I will cherish my time in this beautiful corner of the Essex/Suffolk border, with its cycle of life and renewal, the changes of the seasons and the gentle pride and passion for the area that I share with of so many of its inhabitants. Projects such as the Dedham Vale and Stour Valley Area of Outstanding Natural Beauty highlight the need for people to live, work in and enjoy the valley whilst sharing it with wildlife that must be allowed space to thrive. We are all lessened by the loss of our connection with the natural world, a danger that looms ever larger as our towns and cities groan under the political drive for housing in the south-east. Essex is not 'gently undulating and uninteresting'. There is a balm for all ills here if we only delve deep enough to find and nurture it. I'm eternally grateful it found me so early in life.

Darren Tansley

i.

A new structure had been inserted into the ruins of a dovecote overlooking the marshes. Windows set into the original brick structure were in decay and vegetation was taking over. When the eating of pigeons – which may have been popularised in Britain by the Romans – was more common, the building of a dovecote on a country estate was a sign of self-sufficiency. We looked upwards as grey clouds closed in.

Deep Traces

Under the walled part of Colchester there are deposits, up to about three metres down, that contain the remains of the history of the town over almost the last two thousand years. The Roman remains are in a layer around a metre thick and it's a three-dimensional puzzle down there – you get layers and pits and trenches. Sometimes the Roman deposits are quite near the surface, maybe only half a metre down, particularly along the High Street.

In the very bottom you get the remains of the military fortress that was built in around AD40, for Claudius's visit with the army. The fortress was big enough for five thousand men and it occupies two thirds, maybe slightly more, of the walled part of the town. When you search for this you find the walls and the trenches they dug for the barrack blocks and other buildings. The fortress was a highly organised settlement and although all fortresses were a similar kind of design, all were slightly different from each other. In the middle of it you get the headquarters building and in Colchester that lies pretty much under the Williams & Griffin department store. You then get roads crossing north–south, east–west, which were made from very hard-packed gravel. Sometimes you can still see the actual camber of the road. They would resurface the roads by adding more and more gravel, and gradually the ground level would be caused to rise. And when they built a new house they quite often didn't clear away the remains of the previous building and, again, everything gradually gets higher and higher – which is good for archeologists.

When the legion was withdrawn they kept lots of the buildings and converted them into suitable accommodation and government buildings for the new town – and that was the town that Boudicca destroyed in AD61. We can tell that the destruction was pretty comprehensive. Everywhere we dig we find the remains of Boudiccan destruction and it really dominates the archeological remains. Of the metre thick layer, sometimes half of it or more is taken up with remains of the Boudiccan destruction and in this you get a lot of interesting and unusual discoveries. The houses were made of clay bricks, but not fired, just dried. In the heat of the fire that destroyed the town they were hardened into really solid bricks and their shape was preserved beautifully. We find stumps of walls and can tell how they were made, sheets of collapsed and painted wall plaster, floors that have turned from red and chocolate brown to black in the heat of the fire. Under Williams & Griffin we've found organic materials. Foodstuffs, for example, if are allowed to just smoulder rather than being burnt away, will survive. We've discovered figs and dates – obviously imported and not grown in Britain – and wheat.

Along with the fact that it's such a fascinating group of objects, the recent find of a Roman woman's jewellery is so interesting because it has a human story written all over it. As Colchester was attacked by the British in the revolt, the woman and her family and servants retreated to find refuge in the Temple of Claudius. She dug a small pit, not much more than small hole really, just wide enough to stuff in her gold and silver ornaments, her jewellery, some coins and what we think is a small silver jewellery box. She was obviously thinking that she was going to be able to come back and find it – which never happened. We found the jewellery in a room where the destruction had been quite dramatic. Shelves had collapsed, food was scattered about.

The looped gold armlets we found are very similar to ones discovered in Pompeii. In the room we also found around fifty or so little balls, pellets really, about two centimetres across, which are what are known as blue frit – made in Italy and ground up for painting walls blue. It's another Italian – not just Roman – connection. There could have been lots of Italian people in Colchester at the time and she was probably one of them.

Despite the mayhem of the Boudiccan destruction, Colchester's roads were recovered afterwards – the street plan remained much the same – and even pre-Boudiccan building plots began to be used again. New clay brick houses were built, although these didn't last very long and were replaced within around fifty years, this time with more substantial and larger buildings with better foundations and occasionally stone walls. These buildings tended to last several hundred years.

In the third century AD the town reached its maximum prosperity – we can judge this by the number and size of houses. But then by the late third century a lot of the houses were knocked down and big spaces began to appear in the town. By the end of the fourth century there was quite a lot of empty space in the walled town. In the fifth, Anglo-Saxon buildings appear – little huts, thinly scattered – that are a completely alien approach to housing for Colchester. The Anglo-Saxon buildings are hard to find. They tended not to bring building materials in from outside and they didn't leave much behind.

It's only in the tenth century that Colchester started to take off again as a town. You start to see a more substantial build-up of layers in the ground and by the late Medieval period you find lots of glazed pots and glassware. We find brick houses replacing timber framed ones. The layers under Colchester are quite complicated. Under Williams & Griffin we discovered the remains an iron foundry that dates from the late eighteenth century. It all adds to the colour of the whole. Outside of the walled town are the streets that led up to the town gates, with houses along the approach – ribbon development. The gates were still used up to the seventeenth century. Further out you get the cemeteries of the Roman period. At the garrison we've excavated over a thousand burials and there's a great variety in the way people are buried and what's buried with them. We can build up a picture of the people from these items and from the bones as well. It's a rich source of evidence for what kinds of people lived there.

In many ways, from the Medieval period onwards,

Colchester is rather typical of towns across Britain, but in the Roman town there are lots of things that you don't discover elsewhere. But it's the Boudiccan remains, and those of the fortress, that are very important if you want to study how town life began in Britain. There are still things to be found. For example, we still don't know where the public baths were, or the forum and basilica. There should be an amphitheatre too. While we pretty much know the street system, we don't know what happened in all of the squares. What we think we know now might of course be proved to be wrong by future archeologists. Archeologists are getting better and better at understanding what they're digging and they'll dig better and better too. There's an argument that you should dig as little as possible now to save things for the future when we'll know more. They might come up with a better explanation – or maybe even the correct one.

Philip Crummy

00

Southminster, Essex, 1978

The Seiko LC Digital Quartz Memorybank FX 003 caliber M354 calendar watch of 1978 has some claim to being the world's first smartwatch. It featured an eighty-year calendar that users could set with reminders for specific days. During his acting pomp as fictional British spy James Bond, Roger Moore wore one of the watches in the 1979 film *Moonraker*. I remember the older brothers of classmates at school describing the Memorybank as a computerised watch but I didn't listen properly and I misunderstood. In my mind it was a 'Memoryblank' watch – a one-off device developed by the British Secret Services that could erase thoughts from enemy agents. Our family was in Northumberland during *Moonraker*'s cinematic release. The previous year, a year sans-Bond, we were in Essex.

The last James Bond movie we had seen as a family, at what we then still called The Pictures, was *The Spy Who Loved Me*, a film that bore little resemblance to the book that was its inspiration. Ian Fleming's short 1962 novel was written as the writer tired of 007. His narrator is Vivienne Michel, who also gets a co-author credit, and Bond only appears some way into the text. The book was banned in some countries for its sexually explicit content. In the United States an abridged version of the story appeared in the magazine *Stag*, under the title 'Motel Nymph'.

James Bond would surely never be seen in a motel, but to a child in Britain in the 1970s, motels appeared glamorous. Their proximity to still-gleaming, three-laned motorways, the sleek horizontality of their architecture, the indeterminate edgelands that surrounded them, spoke of frontier towns, of wildly bearded truckers transporting unverified cargoes, of abbreviated resting places for businessmen with no time to lose: they spoke of oil and mileage, of speed, of modernity, of America.

I spotted motel signs from the rear window of a Chrysler Avenger on family trips, punctuating Britain's proto new-world landscape from Gretna Green to Tiverton. In my mind, I remember one on the outskirts of a town somewhere near Braintree – a small, low building with some cart wheels propped up outside next to some gas canisters or milk churns and an almost empty car park. It might have been the Barn Motel, famed for the murder of Muriel Patience in 1972 and the shooting of her husband and daughter. George Ince was tried for the murder at Chelmsford Crown Court. He was found innocent, but his alibi left him in something of a serious predicament: it was reported he had spent the night in question with Dolly Kray, the wife of London gangster Charlie, the elder brother of the Kray Twins. Dolly testified in Ince's defence, however, and the true murderer was eventually traced, almost by accident, to a small-time crook in the Lake District, from where my family and I had travelled to

Essex in 1978.

We stayed at a small red-brick cottage, built in the Flemish style, on the edge of an apple orchard somewhere near Southminster. For some weeks in 1978 we had the heat of what might be described as a '1976 summer'. In my mind, our holiday in Essex felt like it was a year out of time. The sun strained our eyes and danced off the water at Burnham-on-Crouch. Maldon was a steep hill and an endless promenade park. We picked windfalls from the almost bare earth under the orchard trees and travelled to Liverpool Street by train for a tiring walk through a baking Hyde Park. The blue and yellow painted livery of British Rail carriages was peeling and faded. I had never been on a train before. I decided yellow was an emblematic colour for the whole of the holiday. Inside the dark of our cottage, there were a small number of paperbacks. One of them was *The Spy Who Loved Me*, its pages yellow, its cover illustrated with a carnation and a knife, set on a background of pale cream.

Blakeney and Wells-next-the-Sea, 1983

A picture of the clipper ship Albatros at Wells-next-the-Sea reminded me of having seen a famous sailing ship moored in a Norfolk harbour during 1983 when I was twelve years old. I had long associated clipper ships with notions of privateering and the transportation of cargoes – including rum, tobacco and, sadly, slaves – across the Atlantic between Europe, Africa, the Caribbean and the

Americas. But the Albatros is a North Sea clipper, built in Denmark, and it never crossed the Atlantic to dock in Jamaica or Antigua. It did sometimes carry human cargo, though: smuggling Jewish refugees out of Nazi Germany to neutral Sweden during the Second World War.

It wasn't the Albatros that I saw in 1983: the ship only arrived in Wells later in the decade. Neither was it the Golden Hind, which I also saw at around that time, but in Devon. Neither was it HMS Victory, whose illustrious commander Horatio Nelson was born in Norfolk, in nearby Burnham Thorpe (and where at Creake Abbey in the 1950s, I recently discovered, Ian Fleming spent some time searching for a buried hoard of treasure). Unfortunately, neither my memory, nor internet research conducted shortly after the East Anglian storm surge late in 2013, provided any conclusive answer as to the ship I had seen in Norfolk thirty years earlier. I started to believe that the ship was not in fact a marine or naval icon anchored for the entertainment of tourists, but simply a tall ship passing through, perhaps one of any number of barques, brigs, clippers, full rigged ships and schooners that over the years might have docked temporarily in places such as Wells.

On the same day we visited Wells in the early 1980s, we drove to Blakeney. It was a humid day and almost sunset when we arrived and, by the time we had parked the car near the quay, we had spotted the sprawling, coal-black cloud that filled the sky to the north. Soon the rain hammered loudly on the roof of our rusting Saab and we quickly pulled cagoules over our heads as we raced along the street seeking shelter and an evening meal. In a small restaurant we ate rainbow trout and plaice by candlelight, admiring the show of thunder and lightning that had severed Blakeney's electricity supply for the evening. While I remember the fish, the gingham tablecloths and the welcoming and jovial staff, I have no recollection of name of the restaurant, and to see pictures of the Blakeney Hotel, White Hart and Kings Arms today – at one of which we must have eaten – brings no enlightenment.

Strangely, my clearest memory of that trip to Norfolk is of buying a pair of grey trainers in a sports shop, situated at the bottom of a small hill in Norwich, where the owner taught me a different way of tying laces. That summer I wore the trainers to play cricket with friends, mimicking the batting and bowling styles of the great West Indies team that had recently lost the World Cup to India. The smiling wicketkeeper Jeffrey Dujon and effortlessly graceful fast bowler Michael Holding, both from Jamaica, were our new folk heroes. I also wore those trainers, carefully laced, to watch the James Bond movie *Octopussy* at the cinema, perhaps contemplating the names of Dujon and Holding alongside that of Ian Fleming, who, I had recently learned during news reports about the new film, had lived in a private estate, Goldeneye, in Oracabessa, Jamaica.

Cambridge, 1994

Rain, again. I left a friend's house in Cambridge without

a jacket and by the time I had reached the centre of town from Midsummer Common it was pouring down. It was to be, I decided, either an afternoon in a pub or at the cinema. I opted for the latter and rounded the corner to the little arthouse place to see what was showing. I watched Patrick Keiller's *London*. Later that week I spent an evening sat on Jesus Green drinking warm bottled beer with a group of Brazilian tourists, mostly girls, who were keen to know my opinion of Pierce Brosnan, the actor who had just been announced as the new James Bond. His first film as the MI6 officer was to be *GoldenEye*, the 17th spy film in the series. In fact, only months after our brief discussion, which was beset by barriers of language and inebriation, filming for some scenes of 'James Bond 17' took place on the Nene Valley Railway, thirty miles from where we were sat. I remember the evening as one of those almost surreal episodes that usually only happen in youth. We took photographs on cheap cameras, exchanged addresses and promised to write and remember names. We spent a lot of the latter part of the evening feeling the need to hug and kiss goodbye. In the morning I left Cambridge to return to the northeast. The Brazilians were headed to London, then Paris. We must have forgotten each other almost by the time we boarded our trains.

A12, 1996

The A12 has taken many names: Euroroutes E8 (pre-1985) and E30; Britain's Worst Road (due to the number of complaints made about its potholes and regular closure due to roadworks); the Colchester Road; the Ipswich Road; the Great Essex Road. In Roman times it was 'Inter V' on the *Iter Britanniarum* road map of the Antonine Itinerary, a survey designed by Julius Caesar and carried out during the reign of Augustus. Linking London with Great Yarmouth, the modern road was named in 1922 as part of the Great Britain road numbering scheme. It initially ran from Stratford in East London into Essex and East Anglia via Gallow's Corner at Romford. It was subsequently extended to the Blackwall Tunnel, which means the road now links the crossing of the River Yare at Yarmouth with the crossing of the Thames in Poplar, London. In the vicinity of the Blackwall Tunnel, the A102 becomes the A12 at a small neighbourhood park, Jolly's Green, next to a twenty-seven storey residential block built in 1963, the Balfron Tower, designed in the brutalist style by a certain Erno Goldfinger – the architect after whom Ian Fleming named his Bond villain Auric Goldfinger.

At some point late on a June evening in 1996, I travelled along the A12 from Chelmsford to Colchester. Now, every time I pass along this stretch of road, I think of that night. The memory always feels strong at first, but in fact the thought is unclear and the road just a cipher. The van in which I was a passenger in 1996 might have been a minibus. I have no idea who drove, what we talked about, whether a cassette player provided any entertainment. No doubt people were smoking. All I remember is the road, the fields, the verges. We had just played a gig at the Army and Navy, supporting an indie band whose moderately successful best days were already behind them. For our band it was as near to life on the road as it ever got. I know that on the journey I recalled the childhood memory of the motel near Braintree, but couldn't remember the name of the town, unfamiliar as I was with Essex at the time. But I was aware that the memory had started an effortless slide into becoming a simulacrum. It looked the same as ever, but was somehow different, and I knew it. It had become untethered from its own past, perhaps necessarily so if it was to stay with me in the years to come. If it was to live, it first had to die. I thought of the faded blues and yellows of British Rail livery as we travelled the nighttime road where the grey of fields and tarmac blurred together, a monotony broken only by the intermittent glow of orange lamplight. That is how it seems now, in any case. It is sometimes difficult to remember the reality of any situation. Feelings are too forgiving and facts don't suffice, yet both hover around us like mosquitoes on a warm but hazy summer evening, looking to bite.

Wivenhoe, 2008

The illustrator Richard Wasey Chopping died on 17 April 2008. He lived in the Store House on the quay at Wivenhoe with his partner, the landscape painter Denis Wirth Miller, who died in 2010. In December 2005 the couple had become the first in Colchester to enter into a civil partnership. Wirth-Miller's obituary in the *Independent* newspaper mentions the bohemian life of 'jollifications' that the couple enjoyed in Wivenhoe. Pictures on a blog curated by Tom Cull, whose family were friends with the couple, show Chopping and Wirth-Miller in the company of Francis Bacon, who also lived for a time in Wivenhoe. In the town today, fond stories still circulate – and are starting to pass from the sureties of the present into the vagaries of legend.

I had first heard of Chopping as an illustrator of birds and butterflies for children's books. A subsequent search for copies of his *A Book of Birds* and *Wild Flowers*, both from 1944, proved unsuccessful. Chopping is most famous, however, for the illustrations he provided for the dust jackets of Ian Fleming's Bond novels, including one for *The Spy Who Loved Me*: 'What suggests its-self is a juxtaposition of a dagger or a gun and an emblem representing love, rather on the lines of your gun with rose … But what can we use now? How about one of those frilly heart shaped Valentines with a dagger thrust through it? … Or there might be young ivy leaves entwined in a gun, or forget-me-nots,' Fleming wrote in a commissioning letter to Chopping, reproduced on Cull's blog.

Forget-me-nots bloom wildly in the woods at Wivenhoe every spring. You can occasionally spy a goldeneye duck on the Colne river near Chopping's former home. Neither, when I see them, makes me think of Fleming's secret agent. The connections we make between the people, places and events in our lives are personal, often arbitrary.

While I enjoyed watching the Bond films as a child I lost interest sometime in my teens. The Seiko digital watch was replaced by smartphones. But I think of the 'Memoryblank' from time to time – how it could, perhaps, with the swipe of a finger, erase our own memories in the cause of good, wiping from our minds the irrelevant, the contaminated, the ruptured, the eroded and the lifeless thoughts that continue to possess us, to permit us to focus on what is, or was, true.

Kelvedon, 2014

'What can we use now?' asked Fleming. What symbols can be fresh, eye-catching, stimulating, yet also carry a sense of continuity and affirmation? These are the common questions that illustrators such as Chopping face as part of their work. The same goes for writers. How do we unearth the new from the old, the unexpected from the commonplace? We desire to find the emblems, the motifs, that are hardy enough to withstand the inclemencies of time but that are also of their time, and of no other time; that are already out of time, already beyond time.

Every day the commuter train stops at Kelvedon. In late July the fields are golden with corn, a rich yellow that fades almost to a steely white as August treads on. It is on these early morning trains that depart Norwich, Ipswich, Clacton, Braintree and Southend for London, that I am reminded of the early tribes of East Anglia. The people of these outlying lands, often Saxon or Gywre, were foederati for the imperial power: small, roughly organised societies that were bonded via treaties and exchange systems that had been developed to meet the needs of the Roman financiers and military. The Romans gave money; the local tribes helped them fight. Foederati, from the noun *foedus* meaning treaty, is from where we get the word federal. Taking the commuter trains in and out of the capital, however, I imagine the word Anglicised as 'fodder'.

The lands of East Anglia sometimes seem to me as if they are only fodder for time. I think of the trading port of Dunwich and the storms of the thirteenth and fourteenth centuries that wiped it from the map, washing five parishes and six hundred houses into the water. The land, with its temporal structures, its transient, fluctuating populations and their ephemeral cultures, becomes eternal at the point it slips into the sea and disappears. It says goodbye just as it starts to continue – to continue and to live a second life, sinking into the rising blank of memory.

MW Bewick

j.

The Interconnector gas pipeline connects Bacton in Norfolk with Zeebrugge. It is owned by Caisse, a Canadian investment fund, natural gas companies Fluxys and Snam in Belgium and Italy, and Gazprom of Russia, whose chairman is a former Russian Prime Minister. We couldn't see the pipeline, but D____ said she could feel a strange frisson of energy that linked the sea defence walls below us with mainland Europe and beyond.

The Doppelganger II

At Landermere: 1890s

I

"Woman in Doorway".
Framed . Dark. Light
occluded. Fills the frame.
Who's here?
It's only a photograph.
Belonging to nobody.

II

Celeste speaks.   Names.

Has the knowledge.

Serenely.

Enthusiastically.

Briskly.

Brightly.

She teases. Proposes.

Pursues. Summons. Purges.

Eugenie following, to catch her drift.

It ain't on to catch a bird that way   says Eugenie

III

Do the doors adjoin?
A soft footfall. That was later.
The midnight hour. And there's
no record of her name. An anonymous
working woman. One amongst many.
Obliterated.
Absent from the archive.

It's
a vanished way of life
setting understanding
at hazard

IV.

Years later. [1915]

Is this? Real? life. At hand.
Celeste is so tired of huge distances . Slaughter so close.
Just over the horizon.

The guns.
Across the channel, the guns. That's all she hears.
Not in Landermere now.
Trying their luck in Brinkwell.

She wished the sea- barrier away.
She wished herself to know the horror.
The edge. The cut. The stench. All of it.

V

If Eugenie had known what they intended, he would
have gone anywhere to avoid it.
But he was caught up. just the same.
Trapped and harnessed as any horse he'd put to plough.

VI

First they had decimated the oaks and taken the beasts.
But that was before, and now irrelevant.

VII

He was to leave. No avoiding it.
There you go. Bump. he said. Gone. If you're lucky.

Celeste felt goosey. She saw the castle, superimposed. A ruin. Shelled. On the rim of her vision. She saw Eugenie, bayonet fixed. The scene was flooded with light.
She wandered through the debris, poking mounds of bodies with her stick. Searching for clues.

VIII

It was, all of it, a gilded crime: wrapped in lying banners of glory.

IX

Celeste returned.
At the old pub she met the landlady. She resembled Celeste.
Celeste asked the photographer for an image. It was
for Eugenie. When finally the photograph reached her,
it was of a tall woman, of dark complexion, tight-
waisted, in full black skirts, filling the doorway.
Behind her, blurred, the indistinct image of Another.

A ghostly doppelganger? a trick of the print?
Radiating darkness.

X

It was then that she knew Eugenie was dead.

XI

Celeste must persevere alone.
But Celeste was in thrall to the possibility of knowledge.
Knowledge she must have.
Knowledge that would take the shape of Eugenie.
She knew, only too well, such knowledge could elude her.
For now there was no clear way forward.

Her stomach, sickeningly full, rose to her throat. She could not speak. It spilled out , through her; she felt herself to be conduit. She could not avoid the gash it made. There was a tear in the fabric. Night would be pitiless.

XII

Writing in books now could not armour her.
Nothing moved.

It may be it is the death of love holding her to ransom.
There is no Eugenie. No child. She is alone.
She cannot pay the price. The cut is made.
It will not match up.

***

Each must find the best ending of which they are capable.
It all tends towards that.
The best ending possible.
She stands framed in the dark doorway.
Behind her the peopled darkness. Ahead of her
emptyness.

Wendy Mulford

This tale is derived from a photograph of a woman
in the doorway of The Kings Head, Landermere, Anon.
n/d, hanging in the studio of the painter Luke Elwes
at Landermere.

ABOUT THE AUTHORS

MELINDA APPLEBY is an East Anglian writer who explores connections between the nature and culture of land, and our relationship with it. Melinda won *Country Living*'s Best Writer Award in 2011. She has a Creative Writing Diploma from University of East Anglia and has recently completed an MA in Wild Writing from the University of Essex. Her poems have been published in a fenland anthology and *Earthlines*.

MW BEWICK is a writer, editor, journalist and musician, but not always in that order. He grew up in the Lake District and has since lived in Sheffield, Durham, Essex, London and Essex again. He is a former literary manager of the Blue Elephant Theatre, London and as a singer-songwriter released a solo single and an EP with Acertone on Hard Graft records. He is a co-founder of Dunlin Press and his flash fiction can be found at mwbewick.wordpress.com.

EDMUND BLAKENEY is a budding writer and poet and is a recent graduate of English Literature from the University of Essex. He has lived most of his life in Norfolk and is fascinated by the obscure and marginal literary heritage of East Anglia and by the 'hidden treasures' of English folklore.

JAMES CANTON has taught on the MA in Wild Writing at the University of Essex since its inception in 2009 and has run many workshops to encourage writing on nature and landscape. His first book, *From Cairo to Baghdad: British Travellers in Arabia* was published in 2011. His latest work *Out of Essex: Re-Imagining a Literary Landscape* (2013) is inspired by rural wanderings in the county.

PHILIP CRUMMY was born in Edinburgh. He is a member of the Institute for Archaeologists and the director and chief archaeologist of the Colchester Archaeological Trust, a registered charity founded in 1963 to research into and promote the archaeology of Colchester. He received an honorary doctorate from the University of Essex in 2008.

TIM CUNNINGHAM is an Irish poet who lives in Essex. His collections, *Don Marcelino's Daughter* (2001) and *Unequal Thirds* (2006) were published by Peterloo Poets; *Kyrie* (2008), *Siege* (2012) and *Almost Memories* (2014) by Revival Press.

IVAN CUTTING helped found Eastern Angles in 1982 and is now its chief executive and artistic director. The company is a National Portfolio Organisation of the Arts Council and creates theatre with a sense of place. He has also written many of its plays, including in 2012 *Private Resistance* and in 2015 *Oysters*. For Radio 4 he wrote and directed *The Reapers Year.* He regularly contributes to the Birkbeck MFA Director's course, is a Fellow of Suffolk New College, a Trustee of the East Anglian Traditional Music Trust, a director of New Heritage Solutions and was awarded an Honorary Doctorate by UEA/University College Suffolk in 2004.

MARK DEAL is a sound recordist, working between the field and the studio. An Essex-native, Mark aims in his sound work to provide a sense of what it was like to be in place (real or imagined) at a specific place and time. His website is at veryreverend.com.

LUKE ELWES is a painter whose work has been exhibited widely in the UK and Europe since his first exhibition in 1990. He currently divides his time between the studio in London and the marshes, islands and creeks on the Essex coast.

ELAINE EWART is a poet and nature writer who recently completed an MA in Wild Writing: Literature and the Environment at the University of Essex. She was the first Fenland Poet Laureate in 2012, and her first short poetry collection, *Fur, Feather and Fen*, was self-published in 2014. She blogs at flightfeather.wordpress.com.

DR TIM GARDINER is an ecologist and poet. His haiku have been published in literary magazines including *Blithe Spirit, Frogpond* and *Presence.* His first collection of poetry, *Wilderness,* is to be published by Brambleby Books. He has published many papers on natural history and several books, including one about glow-worms.

LANDER HAWES is a writer whose novel *Captivity* was published by Unthank Books in 2012. His story 'Bird Tables for Swans' was shortlisted for the Bridport Prize 2014, and 'Differences in Lifts' appeared in *Unthology 2.* He has read at events in London, Norwich and at the Short Wonder Short Story festival. He lives and works in Norwich, and is on twitter at @landerhawes.

ROBERT JACKSON was born Cheltenham in 1944 and between 1962 to 1967 studied at the Slade School of Fine Art in London. Between 1967 and 1969 he lived in a barn at Pattles Farm, Knodishall, Suffolk and moved into the former Primitive Methodist Chapel, Westleton in 1977. There, as Westleton Chapel Gallery, he mounted art exhibitions from 1979 to 1991, and in 1982, as Chapel Books, began selling rare and secondhand books. In 2009 he launched chapelbooks.com.

ANTONY JOHAE has been based in Colchester since the 1950s. He has a Ph.D in Comparative Literature and has taught at the University of Essex, and in West and North Africa and the Middle East. He is now writing freelance and divides his time between Lebanon, where his wife comes from, and Colchester.

ELLA JOHNSTON is an artist, illustrator, journalist and crafter. Her drawings and paintings are often engagements with the natural world and have been shown in London and across the southeast. Recent illustrations have appeared in magazines including *Firewords Quarterly* and *The Eighty-Eight.* Ella was born in London and lives in Wivenhoe, Essex. Ella is a co-founder of Dunlin Press. See her work at ellajohnston.wordpress.com

PETER KENNEDY says that while poetry might be experiencing a resurgence in popularity, for him it has never gone away. Retirement from the medical profession allowed Peter to rekindle his early love for poetry and writing poetry and, although 'much advanced in years', he says he is still trying to find his voice. Peter also runs Poetry Wivenhoe.

POPPY KLEISER was the Fenland Poet Laureate for 2014. She attempts through both written and spoken word to explore the secrets of the radical and haunting place she lives. She has performed widely; from festivals to exhibitions and shows about land rights history.

THYRZA LEYSHON lives and works in Essex. Her poetry is often concerned with an exploration of place and identity derived from her Welsh roots, West Country upbringing and her response to the flatlands of the East. Her work has been published in a variety of poetry magazines.

CHRIS MAILLARD is a wordsmith for hire, for pleasure and for lack of other options. Also uncomplicated cook, deeply average guitarist, vaguely competent bicycle builder, occasionally successful gardener, secret graphic designer, emergency photographic assistant, parent, peasant, pest. Hangs his mildly Dylanesque hat in the East of London and the South of Norfolk.

ADRIAN MAY's newest project, 'The Ballad of John Ball and Brian Bird', comprises songs/poems about the Peasant's Revolt and local Reverend Bird who wrote about Ball (1980s) and about Skiffle (1950s). His most recent CD/ book is *Comedy of Masculinity* (Wivenbooks). Read Adrian's Writing Shed at makingtextessex.wordpress.com/adrains-writing-shed

LAURENCE MITCHELL is a travel writer and photographer who, despite a penchant for border zones and territories in transition like Central Asia and Eastern Europe, also enjoys exploring and writing about places closer to his home in Norfolk. His blog can be found at eastofelvedon.wordpress.com.

WENDY MULFORD grew up in Wales, has has lived in London, Cambridge and Suffolk and has taught in Cambridge and London (latterly at Anglia Ruskin and Cambridge universities) for 30 years. She founded the influential poetry press Street Editions in 1971. *And Suddenly, Supposing: Selected Poems* was published by Etruscan Press in 2002 and *The Land Between* was published by Reality Street in 2009. Recent work has appeared in *By the North Sea: An Anthology of Suffolk Poetry*, edited by Aidan Semmens (Shearsman, 2013) and she has also contributed to *In Her Own Words: Women Talking Poetry and Wales*, edited by Alice Entwistle (Seren 2014).

MARTIN NEWELL is a musician and writer. He makes records and writes books. He has written for the *Independent* titles, the *Guardian*, *Mojo*, *Record Collector*, *Viz* comic and other titles. He is currently the Saturday columnist for the *East Anglian Daily Times* and resident poet for the *Sunday Express*. He lives in Essex where he divides his time.

CHRIS PETIT is a novelist and filmmaker. During the 1970s he was film editor for *Time Out* and wrote for the *Melody Maker*. His 1979 road movie *Radio On* is considered a cult classic. Novels include *Robinson* (1993), *The Hard Shoulder* (2001) and *The Passenger* (2006).

ROSIE SANDLER lives near Maldon in Essex. Her poetry has been published in, among others, *The Rialto*, *The Poetry of Sex (*Penguin, 2014) and the *Anthology of Dance* (Emma Press, 2015). She was a prizewinner in the 2014 Folio/Bramley Apple Festival poetry competition and was commended in the 2014 Poetry Wivenhoe poetry competition. She was an official reader at the 2014 Essex Poetry Festival.

DAVID SOUTHWELL is an Essex boy and also a landscape punk, photographer, folklorist and author who has written 'several crimes against dead trees'. He now makes amends for this by taking the advice given to him by JG Ballard, to 'concentrate on place, nothing without a sense of it is ever any good'.

DARREN TANSLEY spent an 'idyllic childhood' on the Essex/Suffolk border. In his twenties he travelled the world as a musician. On returning to East Anglia, and gaining a degree in Conservation Management, he joined Essex Wildlife Trust and now spends his life protecting wildlife and habitats in the countryside he loves.

JENNIFER WALFORD lives in Clacton-on-Sea and her ambition is to establish a career in writing. In her early forties she rekindled a childhood amusement by enrolling on a Creative Writing course. During the three-year degree, the 'elusive genre' of psychogeography inspired her to write *Three Sorts of Sunshine*. Jennifer is currently studying for an MA in Literature at the University of Essex.

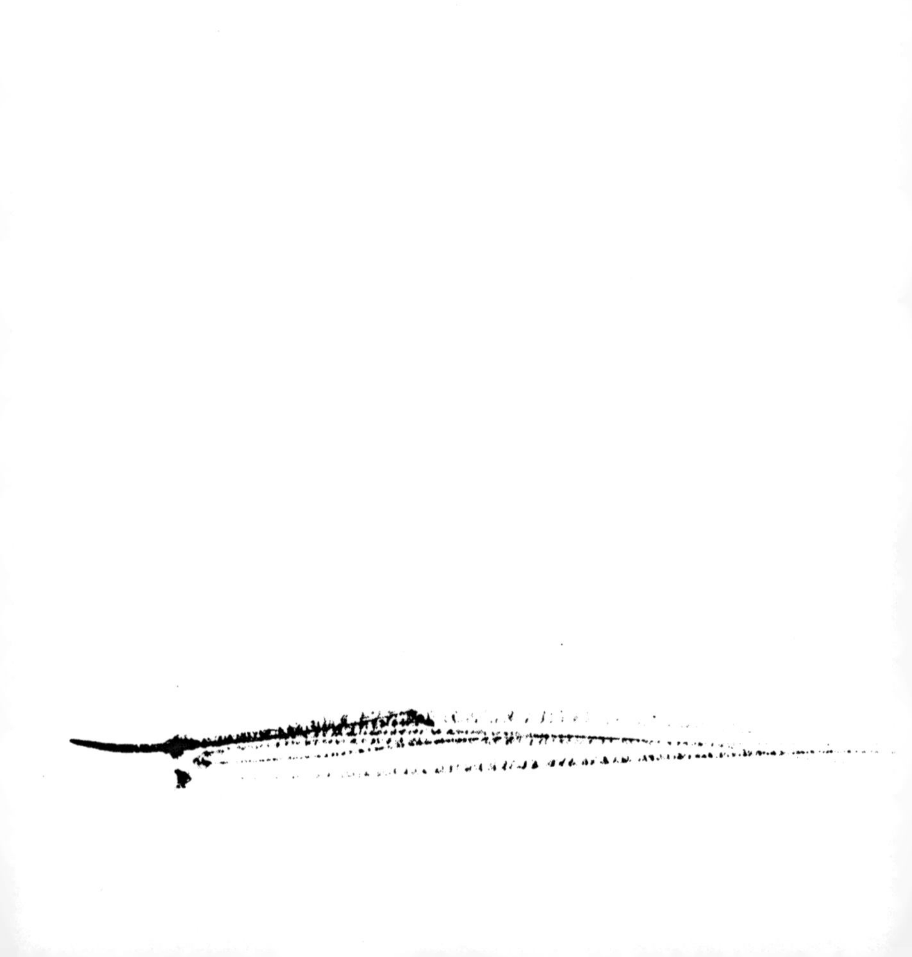

INDEX OF PLACES

Lightning Source UK Ltd.
Milton Keynes UK
UKOW02f1907091116
287295UK00001B/26/P

9 780993 125904